First Workshop on Language Technology for Digital Humanities in Central and (South) –Eastern Europe 2017

Held in Conjunction with Recent Advances in Natural Language Processing (RANLP 2017)

Varna, Bulgaria
8 September 2017

ISBN: 978-1-5108-5544-1

Printed from e-media with permission by:

Curran Associates, Inc.
57 Morehouse Lane
Red Hook, NY 12571

Some format issues inherent in the e-media version may also appear in this print version.

Printed by Curran Associates, Inc. (2018)

Association for Computational Linguistics
209 N. Eighth Street
Stroudsburg, Pennsylvania 18360

Phone: 1-570-476-8006
Fax: 1-570-476-0860

acl@aclweb.org

Additional copies of this publication are available from:

Curran Associates, Inc.
57 Morehouse Lane
Red Hook, NY 12571 USA
Phone: 845-758-0400
Fax: 845-758-2633
Email: curran@proceedings.com
Web: www.proceedings.com

RANLP 2017

Workshop in conjunction with
Recent Advances in Natural Language Processing (RANLP)
2017

Proceedings of the First Workshop on Language technology for Digital Humanities in Central and (South-)Eastern Europe LTDH4CSEE

First Workshop on
Language technology for Digital Humanities in Central and
(South-)Eastern Europe

PROCEEDINGS

Varna, Bulgaria
8 September 2017

Designed and Printed by INCOMA Ltd.
Shoumen, BULGARIA

The workshop was supported partially by the Volkswagen Foundation through the Project HercoRe.

Introduction

During the last decades Digital Humanities evolved dramatically, from simple database applications to complex systems involving most recent state of the art in Computer Science. Especially Language Technology plays a major role either for processing the metadata of recorded objects or for analyzing and interpreting content Applying language technology methods to objects from humanities is a challenge for NLP-research: data is heterogenous (image /text), often incomplete (e.g. OCR errors), multilingual within one document (historic documents with Latin or /and classical Greek paragraphs) and difficult to structure (paragraphs, titles, pages are somewhat different in historical texts).Corpus-based methods, nowadays standard in NLP research cannot be often applied as the necessary large training data is missing. Moreover requirements of tools for digital humanities, especially such tools dedicated to cultural heritage objects are different from those for tools applied to modern texts. Thus performing research in Digital Humanities involves also adapting existent NLP Tools for historical variants of languages, developing tools for new languages, making tools robust for syntactic deviation and adapting semantic resources.
Central and Eastern Europe was always characterized by a high concentration of languages and cultures. Unfortunately, especially here many historical documents are in bad condition; many languages or dialects became extinct over the time and their written evidence is rare. Digital Humanities seems the perfect means for preservation and investigation of this rich cultural heritage asset. However, up to now, dedicated activities seem to miss, probably also due to the lack of adequate NLP resources and tools. Thus it is imperiously necessary to evaluate existent technology, monitor current activities, network research teams in this area, all aims of proposed workshop.

The papers selected for presentation address various topics of Digital Humanities research: linguistics, history, literary, politics or education. Ludmila Malahov, Cătălina Mărănduc and Alexandru Colesnicov describe the process of building a diachrone corpus for Romanian language while Victoria Bobicev, Cătălina Mărănduc and Cenel Augusto Perez report about the design and implementation of tools for the analysis of such diachrone corpus. In Multilingual Ontologies for the Representation and Processing of Folktales, Thierry Declerck and his colleagues focus on the acquisition of ontologies and their usage for the analysis of literature, on particular folklore. Annotation and interpretation of vague expressions in historical texts is discussed in the paper of Anca Dinu, Walther v. Han and Cristina Vertan. Methods from language technology applied for education are reported in the contribution of (among others) Maria Stambolieva . Finally Cristina Moise show how political studies can benefit from computational approaches.

We hope that the paper selection will get a first glimpse of ongoing research activities in the field of Digital Humanities in Central and Eastern Europe and will encourage other researchers to report about their results and build communication networks, following the model in e.g. German speaking, countries. We would like to thank the organisers of the RANLP conference who gave us the opportunity to organize for the first time a workshop on DH dedicated to Central and Eastern Europe Countries, as well as members of the Programme Committee who provided valuable feed-back to all contributions.

September 2017

Anca Dinu, Petya Osenova, Cristina Vertan

Organizers:

Anca Dinu, University of Bucharest, Romania
Petya Osenova, Bulgarian Academy of Sciences, Bulgaria
Cristina Vertan, University of Hamburg, Germany

Program Committee:

Livu Dinu, University of Bucharest, Romania
Antske Fokkens, Vrjie University, Amsterdam
Walther v. Hahn, University of Hamburg, Germany
Vladislav Kubon, Charles University Prague, Czech Republic
Maciej Ogrodniczuk, Polish Academy of Sciences, Poland
Gabor Proszeky, Pázmány Péter Catholic University, Budapest, Hungary
Kiril Simov, Bulgarian Academy of Sciences, Bulgaria
Stefan Trausan, Politechnica University Bucharest, Romania

Table of Contents

Conference Program

9:30–9:45	*Welcome* Anca Dinu, Petya Osenova, Cristina Vertan
9:45–10:30	*Digital Humanities : Current Trends and Challenges for CEE* Cristina Vertan
10:30–11:00	***Coffee Break***
11:30–12:00	*A Diachronic Corpus for Romanian (RoDia)* Ludmila Malahov, Cătălina Mărănduc and Alexandru Colesnicov
12:00–12:30	*Tools for Building a Corpus to Study the Historical and Geographical Variation of the Romanian Language* Victoria Bobicev, Cătălina Mărănduc and Cenel Augusto Perez
12:30–14:00	***Lunch***
14:00–14:30	*Multilingual Ontologies for the Representation and Processing of Folktales* Thierry Declerck, Anastasija Aman, Martin Banzer, Dominik Macháček, Lisa Schäfer and Natalia Skachkova
14:30–15:00	*On the annotation of vague expressions: a case study on Romanian historical texts* Anca Dinu, Walther von Hahn and Cristina Vertan
15:00–15:30	*Language Technologies in Teaching Bugarian at Primary and Secondary School Level: the NBU Platform of Language Teaching (PLT)* Maria Stambolieva, Valentina Ivanova, Mariana Raykova, Milka Hadjikoteva and Mariya Neykova
15:30–16:00	***Coffee Break***
16:00–16:30	*NATURAL LANGUAGE PROCESSING IN POLITICAL CAMPAIGNS* Cristina Moise
16:30–17:00	*Discussions and Concluding Remarks* Anca Dinu, Petya Osenova, Cristina Vertan

A Diachronic Corpus for Romanian (RoDia)

Ludmila Malahov
Institute of Mathematics
and Computer Science of
the Academy of Sciences
of Moldova - Chisinau
Republic of Moldova
lmalahov@gmail.com

Cătălina Mărănduc
Faculty of Computer Science,
"Al. I. Cuza" University
Iasi, Romania
Academic Institute of Linguistics
"Iorgu Iordan Al. Rosetti",
Bucharest, Romania
catalinamaranduc@gmail.com

Alexandru Colesnicov
Institute of Mathematics
and Computer Science of
the Academy of Sciences
of Moldova - Chisinau
Republic of Moldova
acolesnicov@gmx.com

Abstract

This paper describes a Romanian Dependency Treebank, built at the Al. I. Cuza University (UAIC), and a special OCR techniques used to build it. The corpus has rich morphological and syntactic annotation. There are few annotated representative corpora in Romanian, and the existent ones are mainly focused on the contemporary Romanian standard. The corpus described below is focused on the non-standard aspects of the language, the Regional and the Old Romanian. Having the intention to participate at the PROIEL project, which aligns oldest New Testaments, we annotate the first printed Romanian New Testament (Alba Iulia, 1648). We began by applying the UAIC tools for the morphological and syntactic processing of Contemporary Romanian over the books first quarter (second edition). By carefully manually correcting the result of the automated annotation (having a modest accuracy) we obtained a sub-corpus for the training of tools for the Old Romanian processing. But the first edition of the New Testament is written in Cyrillic letters. The existence of books printed in the Old Cyrillic alphabet is a common problem for Romania and The Republic of Moldova, countries where the Romanian is spoken; a problem to solve by the joint efforts of the NLP researchers in the two countries.

1 Introduction

The UAIC-RoDia-DepTb [1] is a balanced corpus of the Dependency treebank type, including all the styles of Romanian, and focusing on non-standard ones. The corpus contains more styles of Romanian, such as folklore, journals, FrameNet translated in Romanian, legal texts (Acquis communitaire), Romanian and foreign fiction, social media (chat) popularization scientific style (Wikipedia), quotations (also poetry). The treebank has now 16,187 sentences, with 322,404 tokens, punctuation included, between which 5,723 sentences in Oold Romanian are also included (99,749 tokens).

Preserving the cultural heritage means not only scanning the old books, so as to prevent their loss by paper damaging. We also need to read and annotate the information contained in the old texts; it needs to be preprocessed, in order to apply to it the programs for information retrieval, for question answering, for machine translations, or for automatic texts resuming, operations in whose absence this information is not accessible to contemporary readers or researchers.

All these operations are based on the POS-tagging or on the syntactic parsing; the texts must be previously annotated on morphological and syntactic information. A POS-tagger for Old Romanian was built, having an accuracy of 91.66%. (Mărănduc et al., 2017).

But the first step to enable processing these old texts is to transform their photos into the editable text format. This step is the most difficult one, because old Romanian texts, although the language has Latin origin, are written in Cyrillic letters of all forms and in all orthographic conventions encountered in the neighboring slave peoples.

Old Romanian is also a non-standard variant of the language, because the rules have not yet been established and each writer applied his own principles to transcribe the spoken language or to change the form of inflected words. The syntactic peculiarities are also very diverse. Building this corpus, we have also built or trained some tools for Roma-

[1] UAIC-RoDia = ISLRN 156-635-615-024-0

Proceedings of the LT4DHCSEE in conjunction with RANLP 2017, pages 1–9,
Varna, Bulgaria, 8 September 2017.

nian language processing; they have a good accuracy percentage for contemporary standard Romanian. A clone of the POS tagger for processing Old Romanian was built, but the syntactic parser has not yet been sufficiently trained on this type of texts.

A first fragment of the New Testament (1648, first edition) was transformed into an editable Cyrillic text by an OCR program that began operating in August 2016. The printed book will be entirely transposed to editable Cyrillic letters and then to the Latin alphabet by the researchers of the Institute of Mathematics and Computer Science of Chisinau; this is the first such operation in practice.

The editable text in the Cyrillic script obtained in the first step of the process was checked by comparing it with the printed old book, and then was wrapped in the XML format, obtaining the second form of the first 2,500 annotated and manually supervised sentences. The Latin form obtained in the second step of the processing was compared with the second edition of the book, manually transposed in Latin letters by priests, without the intention to actualize, or normalize the text.

Our purpose has been to use the entirely annotated and checked book for the extraction of an old lexicon to be introduced in the tools, and also for the training of these tools on Old Romanian. Simultaneously, the work of the regional sub-corpus has begun, with the intention to include, in future, the south Danube dialects of Romanian. The transformation of the syntactic classic treebank in the UD (Universal Dependencies) format and in another semantic format has also begun. The first part of the New Testament, the four Gospels, has been entirely annotated and manually corrected in the classic syntactic format and in the new logical-semantic one.

The Old Romanian sub-corpus will also be a balanced treebank, including not only religious books, but also historical texts (chronicles), legal texts (codices), anonymous folk tales, documents ranged by centuries, and even a cookbook.

The academic Institutes of Linguistics in Iasi and Bucharest have big collections of non-annotated texts in all the styles and from all the periods of the Romanian language evolution. The books are printed and processed by OCR (Optical Character Recognizer) programs. The (non-supervised) texts obtained have more errors in the case of books printed in the 19th century. But books from the sixteenth to the eighteenth centuries, the Romanian texts written in Old Cyrillic alphabets, could not be processed with an accessible OCR program, such as ABBYY Fine Reader 12.

The researchers of Romania and of The Republic of Moldova have the same problem. The two countries constituted a single state in the past, the historical documents (written in Old Cyrillic) are common, and the regional variants of Romanian spoken in the two countries, with minor differences, are mutually understandable.

We have decided to continue together increasing our balanced treebank. Our purpose is to build a big training gold corpus for Old Romanian, to collect the data from it and also to build a variant of our syntactic parser that can automatically process the old text with good accuracy. A lexicon obtained from this corpus has been included in the POS-tagger for Old Romanian and (with Cyrillic letters) in the OCR program. We continue to increase the lexicon in order to augment the accuracy of these tools. We use the bootstrapping method, and the checked sentences are always added to the gold corpus for the training of tools.

2 Directions for Increasing the Corpus

The balanced corpus will be increased by adding a lot of regional variants. For the moment, the introduction of popular regional texts collected in the two countries is in progress, adding the folklore in verse from all the regional variants of Romanian. That is also a non-standard style, because each regional variant of the language has its own regularities, and we must train our tools on each of them.

By introducing in the lexicon of the POS tagger all the lexical or spelling variants of Romanian words, extracted from the Thesaurus Dictionary[2], we introduced in fact the archaic and the regional lexical variants from all over Romania, but we do not know whether there are any variants not included in this dictionary in the Republic of Moldova. Comparisons between the regional peculiarities and statistical studies of differences will become possible. For these comparisons, the sub-treebank of The Republic of Moldova must include other communication styles, for example

[2]http://edtlr.info.uaic.ro/

journalese or fiction.

The annotation of Old Romanian is our priority. We chose to begin with the New Testament of Alba Iulia (1648), the first printed New Testament in Romanian, with the intention of affiliating it to the PROIEL project (Pragmatic Resources in Old Indo-European Languages)[3] (Haug and Johndal, 2008), which aims to align the oldest Latin, Greek, Slavonic and Armenian New Testaments. After the training of tools on this gold corpus, the balanced treebank must be completed with other styles of the old language.

The annotation conventions specific to our treebank will be kept in order to create a very big corpus without inconsistencies, that being the condition for increasing the accuracy of tools on all the language variants. This classic syntactic format is considered the pivot for the transformation into other formats; having a big amount of semantic information, we can develop these new formats and obtain a training corpus for a semantic parser, which will be trained with priority on old Romanian. The transformation into UD (Universal Dependencies)[4] conventions is also in progress, because in this way we can compare our language with the other 30 languages affiliated, but the transformation is accompanied by the loss of one part of the semantic information.

3 Related Work

As regards diachronic corpora, we can cite three recent conferences: the International Conference on Practical Applications of Language PALC Lodz[5], 23-24 October 2015, the Diachronic Corpora, Genre, and Language Change, Nottingham[6] 8-9 April 2016, and the conference Digital Access of Textual Cultural Heritage DATeCH Gttingen, 1-2 June 2017[7].

The need for a research infrastructure for the study of historical textual resources by digitization is increasingly recognized by the historical research community. Historical documents are being digitized on a vast scale in cultural heritage and digital library projects in many countries. Modern linguistics studies increasingly pay attention to diachronic and dialectal variations of languages, studying them with modern formalisms, from the point of view of modern theories. Linguistic studies based on corpora get expanded and grow in importance. Digitized historical corpora are already created for many languages. The pragmatic interpretation of ancient texts is a new direction of research. In the Proceedings of the 12th International Pragmatics Conference in Manchester in 2011 there are chapters based on diachronic pragmatic interpretation of several corpora (Taavitsainen et al., 2014). In Haug and Johndal (2008), the alignment of the oldest New Testament also has a pragmatic purpose. The diachronic corpus of Italian is described in Onelli et al. (2006). There also exist corpora for the dead languages: DCSL (The Diachronic Corpus of Sumerian Literature), a web-based corpus concerning the entire history of the Mesopotamian civilization[8]. There are several papers that describe the creation of diachronic corpora, their purpose, their difficulties, and their usability. A historical American English corpus is presented in Davies (2012); the paper Yanez-Bouza (2011) describes the history of the creation of ARCHER (A Representative Corpus of Historical English Registers), and a multigenre historical corpus. A similar corpus for Old French is described in Martineau et al. (2007). The paper Stein (2008) is a syntactic annotation study for another Old French corpus. Finally, the creation of a German diachronic corpus is described in Dipper et al. (2010). A comparison between the historical Spanish and Portuguese corpora is made in Davies (2010). In Borin et al. (2010), a computational morphological description of Old Swedish is made, and the paper Dipper et al. (2010) is a guideline for the creation of a richly annotated corpus. The paper Martineau et al. (2007) is another guideline, intended for linguists who are uninformed about the perspectives created for their research by linguistic of corpora. We also consulted an entire book collecting papers interested in the corpus based linguistic methods and studies (McEnery et al., 2006).

BLARK (Basic Language Resource Kit) is a software for the research in the field of social-humanities, i. e. a kit for the automatic annotation of resources in this domain (Borin and Forsberg, 2008). East European languages have several preprocessing issues. For example, some of them used Cyrillic and Latin scripts in various

[3]http://www.hf.uio.no/ifikk/english/research/projects/proiel/

[4]http://universaldependencies.org/

[5]http://palc.uni.lodz.pl

[6]https://www.nottingham.ac.uk/conference/fac-arts/clas/dcglc/home.aspx.

[7]http://ddays.digitisation.eu/datech-2017/

[8]http://dcsl.orinst.ox.ac.uk

Figure 1: A fragment of the beginning of the Alba Iulia New Testament (1648)

periods of time; consequently, some documents need to be transliterated before further processing (Gruszczynski and Ogrodniczuk, 2015).

4 The OCR Program for the Old Cyrillic Books

Romanian linguists published a big number of editions with comments for each important book written with Old Cyrillic letters, including their transcription in the Latin alphabet and final indexes or glossaries. But these philological editions are not usable for our purpose. They contain controvertible theories of the sixteenth and seventeenth centuries pronunciation and use an interpretive transcription. The indexes at the end of these books would have been very useful, but if we introduced them in the lexicon of processing tools, they would not find anything in the texts, because the form of the words was an interpretive spelling, or was replaced with the lemma (the form found in contemporary dictionaries). The first printed Romanian New Testament, chosen for beginning the old Romanian gold corpus, is relatively well preserved. (See Figure 1)

Fortunately, the second edition of the Alba Iulia New Testament was published by priests, who did not practice interpretive transcription. We have processed its first 3,000 sentences with our contemporary Romanian tools. The result, whose accuracy is modest, is being carefully manually corrected and will be used to train the tools on Old Romanian. From a philological point of view, this does not mean that we annotate the first New Testament printed in Romanian. The books in


```
<word id="1" form="Нѣмꙋл" lemma="neam" postag="Ncmsry" head="0" chunk="" deprel="" />
<word id="2" form="ши" lemma="şi" postag="Cssp" head="1" chunk="" deprel="coord." />
<word id="3" form="нащерѣ" lemma="naştere" postag="Ncfsry" head="2" chunk="" deprel
="coord." />
<word id="4" form="ал8" lemma="-ul" postag="Tf-so" head="5" chunk="" deprel="det." />
<word id="5" form="Іс" lemma="Iisus" postag="Npmsrn" head="3" chunk="" deprel=
"a.subst." />
<word id="6" form="хс" lemma="Hristos" postag="Npmsrn" head="5" chunk="" deprel=
"a.subst." />
<word id="7" form="кареле" lemma="care" postag="Pw3msry" head="5" chunk="" deprel=
"a.vb." />
<word id="8" form="есте" lemma="fi" postag="Vmip3s" head="7" chunk="" deprel=
"subord." />
<word id="9" form="месіа" lemma="Mesia" postag="Npmsry" head="8" chunk="" deprel=
"n.pred." />
<word id="10" form="фъгъдꙋит" lemma="făgădui" postag="Vmp--sm-p" head="9" chunk=""
deprel="a.vb." />
<word id="11" form="избъвитор" lemma="izbăvitor" postag="Afpmsrn" head="9" chunk=""
deprel="a.adj." />
<word id="12" form="пъринцилор" lemma="părinte" postag="Ncmpoy" head="9" chunk=""
deprel="c.i." />
```


Figure 2: The first sentence of the Alba Iulia New Testament (1648) with Old Cyrillic, annotated in UD conventions Conception and Birth of Jesus Christ, which is the promised Messiah, our parents deliverer.

the PROIEL project are written with their original Greek, Slavonic or Armenian characters. But we did not find another solution to start the project, breaking the vicious circle - we cannot have processing tools because we do not have a training corpus and we cannot have a corpus because we do not have automatic annotation tools.

Then, the researchers at the Institute of Mathematics and Computer Science in Chisinau have been able to process the first portion of the text, with ABBYY FineReader OCR program (AFR), and a specially developed tool pack of add-ons for AFR. It is the first time that a Cyrillic Romanian text of the seventeenth century has been obtained by an OCR program (Colesnicov et al., 2016). AFR has initially been trained on Romanian texts printed after 1945 in The Republic of Moldova with the modern Cyrillic alphabet. In Romania, books were printed with Latin characters starting from the middle of the nineteenth century (due to a law given by the Prince Al. I. Cuza).

The OCR for the Romanian written with Old Cyrillic alphabet is based on the AFR features allowing the introduction of new languages, with their alphabets and lexicons (dictionaries).

AFR has also been trained on texts printed in Romania at the beginning of the nineteenth century, with sufficient good accuracy, something which we cannot hope to achieve for texts of the 17th century. The researchers of Chisinau have processed the print in two steps. In the first step, they obtained an editable form of the book with Old Cyrillic characters (Cojocaru et al., 2017). The computational linguists of Iasi have remarked that three characters are not in the "times_extro" set. Consequently, they are not recognized by the computer, because the set of characters are not all

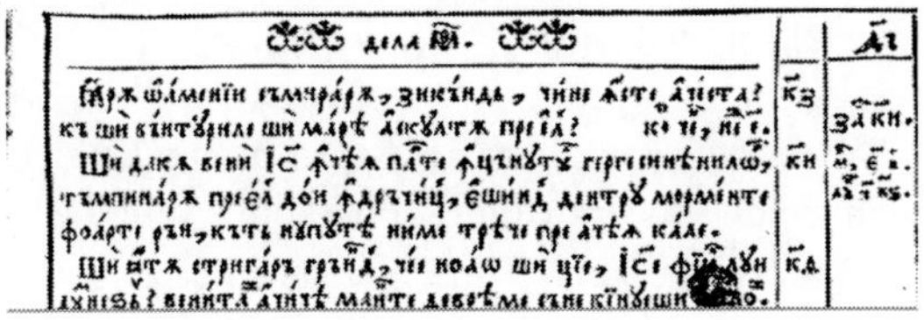

a) The black –white print of the Alba Iulia New Testament

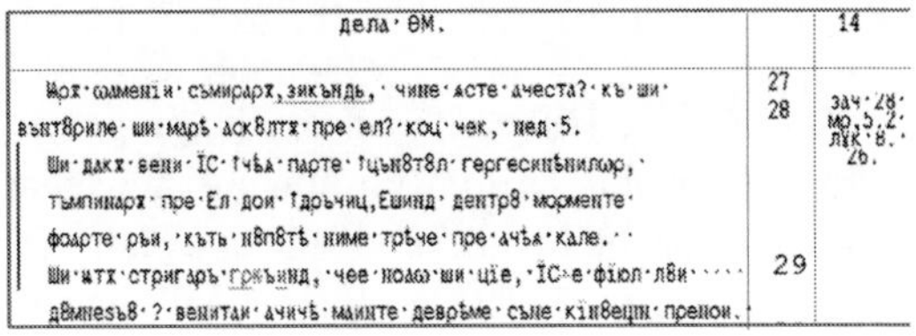

дела · θМ.		14
Ырх · ѡамені и · съмирарх, зикънд ь, · чине · асте · ачеста? · къ · ши · вънт8риле · ши · маръ · аск8лтх · пре · ел? · коц · чек, · нед · 5.	27 28	зач · 28 · мо,5,2 · лук · 8 · 26.
Ши · дакх · вени · ІС · Ічъа · парте · Іцън8т8л · гергесинѣнилѡр, · тъмпинарх · пре · Ел · дои · Ідрьчиц, Ешинд · дентр8 · морменте · фоарте · рьи, · кътъ · н8п8тѣ · ниме · трѣче · пре · ачѣа · кале. · ·		
Ши · атх · стригаръ · гръинд, · чее · ноаѡ · ши · ціе, · ІС · е · фіюл · л8и · · · · д8мнезъ8 · ? · венитаи · ачичѣ · маинте · деврѣме · съне · кіи8ещи · пренои.	29	

b) The editable Cyrillic letters obtained by the OCR

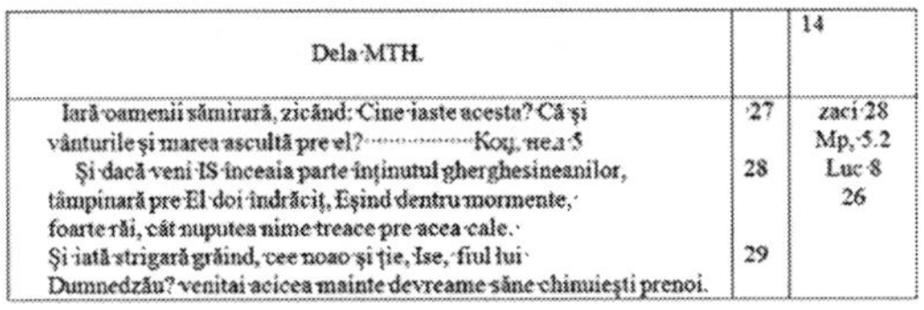

Dela·MTH.		14
Iară·oamenii·sămirară, zicând: Cine·iaste·acesta? Că·și vânturile·și·marea·ascultă·pre·el? ··············Коц, нед·5	·27	zaci·28 Mp,·5.2 Luc·8 26
Și·dacă·veni·IS·inceaia·parte·ințînutul·gherghesineanilor, tâmpinară·pre·El·doi·îndrăciț, Eșind·dentru·mormente,· foarte·răi, cât·nuputea·nime·treace·pre·acea·cale.·	28	
Și·iată·strigară·grăind, ·cee·noao·și·ție, ·Ise, ·fiul·lui· Dumnedzău? ·venitai·acicea·mainte·devreame·săne·chinuiești·prenoi.	29	

c) The transliteration in Latin Letters

Engl. (KJV, Matthew 8): 27. But the men marvelled, saying, What manner of man is this, that even the winds and the sea obey him! 28. And when he was come to the other side into the country of the Gergesenes, there met him two possessed with devils, coming out of the tombs, exceeding fierce, so that no man might pass by that way. 29. And, behold, they cried out, saying, What have we to do with thee, Jesus, thou Son of God? art thou come hither to torment us before the time?

Figure 3: A fragment of the Alba Iulia New Testament (1648)

in the ASCII set. The computational linguists of Iasi replaced the letters with other signs (see Figure 4, first row), and they maintained the letter șc in the form used by the researchers of Chisinau, although it replaces the letter șt, and not șc. With this set of letters, they succeeded in replacing the Latin characters in the checked XML containing the Gospel, the first part of the New Testament. A resulting sentence, annotated in the UD conventions, is shown in Figure 2.

Simultaneously with the replacement of the word form in Latin characters by the word form in Cyrillic characters, the linguists confronted the transcription with the printed book and they signaled the errors of the Chisinau researchers. They encountered more problems:

- A first problem was the numbers of chapters and paragraphs to be preserved. These numbers are universal for any version of the Christian New Testament and essential for the alignment of our New Testament with the other similar books in PROIEL. We decided to introduce them in the general data of each sentence. In the PROIEL project, they were repeated for each word, because in the CONLLU format there is no information about sentences. Our NLP group has built a program for the XML to CONLLU format transposition; there will be added a function to expand the citation part of each word.

Letters not recognized by the ASCHI classification	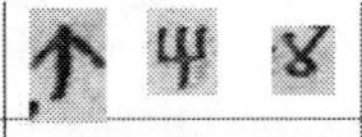	transliteration in actual latin letter: î (or în), șt, u.
Letters digits	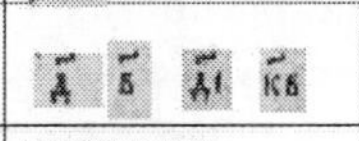	1. 2. 14, 22
Overwritten Letters		mearsără= En: *they walk*; the letter 'r' is overwritten
Overwritten Letters		Esrom (proper noun) the letter 'm' is overwritten
Word whit a stain		Aminadav (proper noun)
Words without a white space between		deîn muiarea En: *from the women*
Abbreviations		Jesus Christ, Mathew (the letter th inside the M)
Transliterations	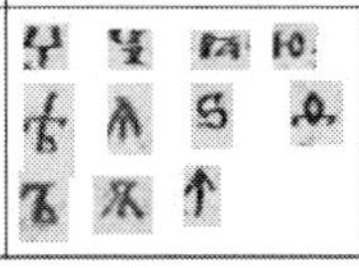	ge, ci/ce, ia, iu, ea/ia, ia, dz, th, ă/â, â/ă, î/în/îm

Figure 4: Some difficulties of the reading and of the transliteration of the Alba Iulia New Testament (1648)

- Therefore, in the printed old books, these numbers are in a separated column and are written with old Cyrillic letters. These signs represent the first paragraph, the second, the third, and so on. (See Figure 4, second row). The list of letters-digits marked by an upper score has been introduced in the OCR program. The letters-digits appear only in the oldest books.

- The OCR must include a splitter that can cross out with spaces the words where they are not separated in the originally printed text, using a big lexicon for old Romanian. For example, in Figure 4, sixth row, there is a string of signs that can be separated, being a preposition, *deîn*, =*de în*, En:*from* and, *muierea* < Lat. mulier. En: *the woman*. This is a specific peculiarity of the first printed books, probably the *white* letter did not yet exist and the letters were placed at various distances that might chance to disappear at the moment when they were pressed, or when orthography respected any rule which we do not know.

- The book contains a lot of abbreviated words. The Chisinau researchers made a list of the individual abbreviations and they wanted the program to replace the abbreviations by entire words. Perhaps this was not compulsory, since abbreviations exist in contemporary languages, too; it is enough to put the list of abbreviations at the beginning of the document. See Figure 4, seventh row.

- Frequently, there are no abbreviated words, but words with some overwritten letters. For example, the word *mearsără* En: *they walk*; the letter "r" is overwritten; the word *Esrom* (proper noun) has an accent and the letter "m" placed over the letter o. see Figure 4, third and fourth row. A solution applied by the OCR authors is to consider each line of text as two lines and to read the overwritten signs, too. But this peculiarity will be a permanent source for decreasing the accuracy percentage and these words must be manually checked.

- Some of the missing letters or words were due to stains. This difficulty could be overcome by giving up the Scan Taylor program (which turned the text black and white, as in Figure 3) and by increasing the resolution. The word Aminadav (proper noun) wasnt entirely recognized by the OCR program reading the black white text, but was recognized reading the color print. See Figure 4, fifth row.

The problem of letters-digit and overwritten is now solved. The output of a book treated by the OCR has some sections, like an invisible table, resembling the printed book that has a division for the notes, the number of chapters, and references of other chapters. In the Figure 3 we have manually traced the table (See figure 3)

5 Some Transcription Difficulties

The second step of the OCR processing created at Chisinau is the transliteration of old Cyrillic letters as Latin characters. The Chisinau researchers have built a POS-tagger that can annotate with morphological information both Romanian texts written with Latin letters and Romanian ones written with modern Cyrillic characters; the program was adopted for old Cyrillic (introducing new characters) and for the operation of transposition (introducing new rules). The computational linguists of Iasi compared the text with Latin letters obtained by the Chisinau researchers with the second edition of the New Testament (used in the automatic morphological and syntactic annotation of the first 3,000 sentences) with Latin characters, obtained by the ABBYY FineReader 12 program. (This program is the starting point for building the OCR for Romanian Old Cyrillic and the specialists from ABBYY helped them with some indications and suggestions.) A fragment of the comparison is shown in Table 1, most of it corresponding to the image (See figure 2).

The bold characters of the table are missing words in the second edition or in the OCR version. The high quality of the first document received from Chișinău is impressive, owing mainly to the careful manual correction of OCR output. The previous examples shows that it was a very difficult task. Some difficulties of transposition of a Cyrillic letter as a group of Latin letters (with more options) are shown in the Figure 4, last row.

The first theoretical observation to be made is that our purpose is to study the peculiarities of the old text, but not to remove them by correcting the text, i.e. by applying rules/norms which did not exist in the studied period of the language evolution. The bishop Simion Stefan was a cultivated man, he was aware of the European ideas of his time, demanding that the religious service and the sacred books be in the language of the people, therefore he wrote without capital letters because in this period there was no rule for the capitalization of proper nouns and of pronouns coreferential with the noun of the Divinity.

Spelling correction is made for the use of a wider audience of non-specialists who are not interested in old books and will probably not read them. On the contrary, the persons interested in the real appearance of the ancient text will not have access to it. We believe we must enter in the lex-

The New Testament (1648), Second Edition, with Latin Letters, Alba Iulia, Romanian Orthodox Diocese Publisher, 1988	**The New Testament (1648), First Printed in Romanian by Simion Ştefan, Bishop of Transylvania, obtained by OCR at IMCS Chişinău**	**The English translation (KJV, Matthew 1:1-17)** Note: different text distribution between verses 10 and 11.
Neamul şi naşterea lui Iisus Hristos carele iaste Mesia făgăduit izbăvitor părinţilor.	Neamul şi naşterea a lui is hs, carele iaste mesia făgăduit izbăvitor părinţilor.	The generation and birth of Jesus Christ, who is the Messiah, promised the savior to the fathers.
1. Cartea de neamul lui Iisus Hristos, fiiul lui David, fiiul lui Avraam.	**1.** Cartea de neamul lui IS hS, fiiul lui david fiiul lui avraam.	1 The book of the generation of Jesus Christ, the son of David, the son of Abraham.
2. Avraam născu pre Isaac, iară Isaac născu pre Iacov, iară Iacov născu pre Iuda şi pre fraţii lui.	**2.** Avraam născu pre Isaac. iară Isaac născu pre Iacov. iară Iacov,născu pre Iuda şi pre fraţii lui.	2 Abraham begat Isaac; and Isaac begat Jacob; and Jacob begat Judas and his brethren;
3. Iuda născu pre Fares şi pre Zara din Tamar, iară Fares născu pre Esrom şi Esrom născu pre Aram.	**3.** Iuda născu pre fares, şi pre zara din Thamar. iară fares născu pre Esrom, şi Esrom născu pre aram.	3 And Judas begat Phares and Zara of Thamar; and Phares begat Esrom; and Esrom begat Aram;
4. Aram născu pre Aminadav, iară Aminadav născu pre Nasson, Nasson născu pre Salmon.	**4.** Aram născu pre amin**adav**. iară aminadav născu pre nasson. nasson născu pre Salmon.	4 And Aram begat Aminadab; and Aminadab begat Naasson; and Naasson begat Salmon;
5. Salmon născu pre Vooz din Rahav, iară Vooz născu pre Ovid din Ruta, Ovid născu pre Isei.	**5.** Salmon născupre vooz diî rahav. iară vooz născu, pre ovid diîrutha . ovid născupre Iesei.	5 And Salmon begat Booz of Rachab; and Booz begat Obed of Ruth; and Obed begat Jesse;
6. Ieseiu născu pre David craiu, iară David craiu născu pre Solomon, den muiarea carea au fost **a** Uriei.	**6.** Ieseiu născu pre david craiu. iară david craiu născu pre Solomon deîn muiarea carea au fost a uriei.	6 And Jesse begat David the king; and David the king begat Solomon of her *that had been the wife* of Urias;
7. Solomon născu pre Rovoam, iară Rovoam născu pre Avia şi Avia născu pre Assa.	**7.** Solomon născu pre rovoam, iară rovoam născu pre avia, şi avia născu pre assa.	7 And Solomon begat Roboam; and Roboam begat Abia; and Abia begat Asa;
8. Assa născu pre Ioasafat, iară Ioasafat născu pre Ioaram şi Ioaram născu pre Oziia.	**8.** Assa născu pre Iosafat, şi Iosafat născu pre Ioaram, şi Ioaram născu pre ozia.	8 And Asa begat Josaphat; and Josaphat begat Joram; and Joram begat Ozias;
9. Oziia născu pre Ioatam, iară Ioatam născu pre Ahaz, iară Ahaz născu pre Ezechiia.	**9.** Ozia născu pre Ioatham, iară Ioatham născu pre ahaz, iară ahaz, născu pre Ezechia.	9 And Ozias begat Joatham; and Joatham begat Achaz; and Achaz begat Ezekias;
10. Ezechiia născu pre Manasia, iară Manasiia născu pre Amon.	**10.** Ezechia născu pre manasia, iară manasia născu pre amon.	10 And Ezekias begat Manasses; and Manasses begat Amon; and Amon begat Josias;
11. Amon născu pre Iosian, iară Iosian născu pre Ehonian şi pre **fraţii lui, în vavlon.**	**11.** Amon născu pre Iosian, iară Iosiae născu pre Ehonian şi pre fraţii lui, în vavlon.	11 And Josias begat Jechonias and his brethren, about the time they were carried away to Babylon:
12. Iară după mutarea în Vavilon, Ehonia născu pre Salatiil, iară Salatiil născu pre Zorovavel.	**12.** iară după mutarea în vavlon, Ehonia născu pre salathiil iarî Salathiil născu pre zorovavel.	12 And after they were brought to Babylon, Jechonias begat Salathiel; and Salathiel begat Zorobabel;
13. Zorovavel născu pre Aviud, iară Aviud născu pre Eleachim, iară Eleachim născu pre Azor.	**13.** Zorovavel născu pre aviud. iară aviud născu pre Eleachim. iară Eleachim născu pre azor	13 And Zorobabel begat Abiud; and Abiud begat Eliakim; and Eliakim begat Azor;
14. Azor născu pre Sadoc, iară Sadoc născu pre Ahchim, Ahchim născu pre Eliud.	**14.** Azor născu pre Sadoc, iară Sadoc născu pre achim, achim născu pre Eliud.	14 And Azor begat Sadoc; and Sadoc begat Achim; and Achim begat Eliud;
15. Eliud născu pre Eleazar, Eleazar născu pre Mattan, iară Mattan născu pre Iacov.	**15.** Eliud născu pre Eleazar. Elea**zar** născu pre matthan. iară matthan născu pre Iacop.	15 And Eliud begat Eleazar; and Eleazar begat Matthan; and Matthan begat Jacob;
16. Iacov născu pre Iosif, bărbatul Mariei, dentru carea născu Iisus, carele Să chiamă Hristos.	**16.** Iacov născu pre Iosif, bărbatul mariei, dentru carea născu IS carele să chiamă hs.	16 And Jacob begat Joseph the husband of Mary, of whom was born Jesus, who is called Christ.
17. Derept acea, toate neamurile de la Avraam pînă la David, patrusprăzeace neamure; şi de la David pînă la mutarea în Vavilon, neamure patrusprăzeace, şi den mutarea den Vavilon pînă la Hristos, neamure 14.	**17.** Derept acea toate neamurile dela avraam până la dvd patrusprăzeace neamure: şi dela dvd până la mutarea învavlon, neamure patrusprăzeace, şi dela mutarea den vavlon până la hS neamure 14.	17 So all the generations from Abraham to David *are* fourteen generations; and from David until the carrying away into Babylon *are* fourteen generations; and from the carrying away into Babylon unto Christ *are* fourteen generations.

Table 1: Comparison between the second edition and the OCR of the New Testament first edition.

icon of processing tools all the forms existing in the old language, in order for them to be recognized and correctly analyzed when found in other texts. For example, if we introduce in the lexicon only capitalized proper nouns, the ones encountered without capitalization will not be correctly annotated.

It is also worth noting that, at that time, the orthographic convention of words joined by a hyphen did not exist. For example, *aflăsă* means *află-se, se află* (En: *there was.*) Therefore, we must annotate two words because the string has the meaning of two words. The inversion of word marks, not used in the contemporary language, is frequently used in ancient texts. Being frequent, the statistical tools will probably be easily trained on it in this respect.

Another big problem is the variety of ancient texts. At different times, in the nineteenth century, there were transition alphabets that mixed Latin letters with Cyrillic letters (Mărănduc et al., 2016). 16 types of transition alphabets were found, classified after the combinations of Latin and Cyrillic letters. There were also differences in the form of letters, and the researchers included in the program an option in which the user can specify the year and the locality where the text was printed. In the sixteenth and seventeenth centuries there were not many locations where books were printed. They introduced in the OCR program different sets of letters, for each of these transitions alphabets and printers.

6 Conclusions and Future Work

After taking the necessary steps for checking the annotation and the OCR obtained by confronting it with the printed book, we can say that we have actually annotated the first printed Romanian New Testament. It is a good idea to compare two transcriptions, (both without the intention to actualize, interpret or correct them), because the text is ancient and difficult. Each of the versions compared has mistaken that the other does not have, and problems better solved than the other. The Chisinau version is as good as the published one. In the meantime, they have solved the problem of the letters digits, which are missing in their version of the table, as can be seen in Figure 3. Any problem that linguists are telling them is solved by the computer scientists in Chisinau. They have reported to ASCHI the characters that are not yet recognized and we are expecting their introduction into international codes. They have also made a set of old Cyrillic letters for Romanian that can be entered on the computer keyboard, and in this way the supervision of results of the OCR will be easier.

The last 2,200 sentences of the Gospel are obtained by the OCR program, and then processed in the same way. And for the second part of the New Testament, i.e. Acts of the Apostles, we intend to introduce the text obtained by OCR in the programs for the automatic morphological and syntactic annotation that will be manually checked. Therefore, the comparison of the second edition must continue. After each step, the programs will be ameliorated by the introduction of the correct information in their lexicon, and by the increase of the training corpus. The OCR will be trained on more printed books with a higher resolution.

We will continue to wrap the gold corpus of Old Romanian with the word form written in Cyrillic letters. We now have 3,000 sentences, we would need more for the training with the Cyrillic variant, to build a POS-tagger which should be able to annotate Romanian ancient texts written in the Cyrillic and Latin alphabets. Perhaps some Romanian linguists will want to study the Cyrillic version of texts, without transposing them into the modern alphabet, as specialists in old Slavic or in old Greek do.

The Chisinau researchers began the study of the problem of the optical character recognition for old Cyrillic letters from some manuscripts. The treebank has now three layers (conventions of annotation). We first annotate each text in the classical syntactic convention that our tools are trained in, and that contains a big quantity of information. It can be automatically transposed in the UD convention, which is the international link between more than 30 treebanks, but has less information. Also the classical syntactic annotation can be automatically transposed in the semantic treebank in proportion of 65%, but the syntactic relation that have a big number of semantic correspondents must be manually annotated. We have transposed in the semantic format the first part (the Gospel) of Alba Iulia New Testament, with the intention to train a semantic parser on this format. The semantic annotated corpus could be aligned with the other old New Testaments in the PROIEL project, and they can import our semantic annotation.

The annotation of the second part of the Alba Iulia New Testament will begin in the coming year. After the full processing and supervision, the New Testament will be transformed in the UD convention and in the CONLLU format and will be affiliated to the PROEL project, which will align it with the other old New Testament versions and the linguists can study the etymology, the translation of old texts, the pragmatic connections between the sentences and other peculiarities. The New Testament will be submitted in four forms: in XML and in CONLLU, with Latin and with Cyrillic characters. Meanwhile, another team will continue increasing the treebank with popular regional texts from all the regions of our two countries. The tools will be trained on each of these non-standardized variants of the language.

References

Lars Borin, Marcus Forsberg, and Dimitrios Kokkinakis. 2010. Diabase: Towards a diachronic blark in support of historical studies. In *Proceedings of LREC*. pages 35–42.

Lars Borin and Markus Forsberg. 2008. Something old, something new: A computational morphological description of old swedish. In *LREC 2008 - Workshop on Language Technology for Cultural Heritage Data (LaTeCH 2008) Conference Proceedings*. pages 9–16.

Svetlana Cojocaru, Alexandru Colesnicov, and Ludmila Malahov. 2017. Digitization of old romanian texts printed in the cyrillic script. In *Proceedings of International Conference on Digital Access to Textual Cultural Heritage*. pages 143–148.

Alexandru Colesnicov, Ludmila Malahov, and Tudor Bumbu. 2016. Digitization of romanian printed texts of the 17th century. In *Proceedings of the 12th International Conference Linguistic Resources and Tools for Processing the Romanian Language*. Alexandru Ioan Cuza University Press, pages 1–11.

Mark Davies. 2010. Creating useful historical corpora: A comparison of corde, the corpus del espanol, and the corpus do português pages 137–166.

Mark Davies. 2012. Expanding horizons in historical linguistics with the 400 million word corpus of historical american english. *Corpora* (7):121–157.

Stephanie Dipper, Lukas Faulstich, Ulf Leser, and Anke Ludeling. 2010. Challenges in modelling a richly annotated diachronic corpus of german. In *Proceedings of the Conference on Language Resources and Evaluation, LREC2010*.

Wlodzimierz Gruszczynski and Maciej Ogrodniczuk. 2015. The electronic corpus of the 17th and 18th century polish texts (up to 1772) aims, methods, current state, problems and prospects for development. In *Slavic Corpus Linguistics: The Historical Dimension*. pages 21–25.

Dag T. T. Haug and Marius L. Johndal. 2008. Creating a parallel treebank of the old indo-european bible translations. In *Proceedings of the Second Workshop on Language Technology for Cultural Heritage Data*. C. Sporleder and K. Ribarov (eds.), pages 27–34.

Cătălina Mărănduc, Ludmila Malahov, Cenel-Augusto Perez, and Alexandru Colesnicov. 2016. Rodia project of a regional and historical corpus for romanian. In *in Proceedings of MFOI*.

Cătălina Mărănduc, Radu Simionescu, and Dan Cristea. 2017. Hybrid pos-tagger for old romanian. In *Proceedings of the International Conference on Computational Linguistics and Intelligent Text Processing (CICLing)*.

France Martineau, Constana Rodica Diaconescu, , and Paul Hirschbühler. 2007. Le corpus voies du francais : de lelaboration à lannotation pages 121–142.

Tony McEnery, Richard Xiao, and Y. Yukio Tono. 2006. *Corpus-based Language Studies: An Advanced Resource Book*. Routledge publisher, London, New York.

C. Onelli, D. Proietti, and C. Seidenari. 2006. The diacoris project: a diachronic corpus of written italian. In *Proceedings of LREC 2006*. pages 1212–1215. http://corpora.dslo.unibo.it/DiaCORIS.

Achim Stein. 2008. Syntactic annotation of old french text corpora. *Corpus* (7):157–172.

Irma Taavitsainen, Andreas H. Jucker, and Jukka Tuominen. 2014. *Diachronic Corpus Pragmatics*. John Benjamins publisher, Amsterdam.

Nuria Yanez-Bouza. 2011. Archer past and present (1990-2010). *ICAME Journal* (35):205–236.

Tools for Building a Corpus to Study the Historical and Geographical Variation of the Romanian Language

Victoria Bobicev
Technical University
of Moldova
Chişinău
Republic of Moldova
victoria_bobicev@rol.md

Cătălina Mărănduc
"Al. I. Cuza" University,
Iasi, Romania
Institute of Linguistics
"Iorgu Iordan Al. Rosetti"
Bucharest, Romania
catalinamaranduc@gmail.com

Cenel Augusto Perez
Al. I. Cuza University,
Iaşi, Romania
augusto.perez@info.uaic.ro

Abstract

Contemporary standard language corpora are ideal for NLP. There are few morphologically and syntactically annotated corpora for Romanian, and those existing or in progress only deal with the Contemporary Romanian standard. However, the necessity to study the dynamics of natural languages gave rise to balanced corpora, containing non-standard texts. In this paper, we describe the creation of tools for processing non-standard Romanian to build a big balanced corpus. We want to preserve in annotated form as many early stages of language as possible. We have already built a corpus in Old Romanian. We also intend to include the South-Danube dialects, remote to the standard language, along with regional forms closer to the standard. We try to preserve data about endangered idioms such as Aromanian, Meglenoromanian and Istroromanian dialects, and calculate the distance between different regional variants, including the language spoken in the Republic of Moldova. This distance, as well as the mutual understanding between the speakers, is the correct criterion for the classification of idioms as different languages, or as dialects, or as regional variants close to the standard.

1 Introduction

The UAIC-RoDia-DepTb (ISLRN 156-635-615-024-0) is a balanced treebank that becomes the core of a big corpus for the Old and Regional Romanian and for its South-Danube dialects. The treebank has now 16,187 sentences, with 322,404 tokens, illustrating all the styles of communication, between which there are 5,723 sentences in old Romanian and 1,230 sentences in regional variants of the Romanian.

If we know the non-standard, regional or earlier forms, we can understand the laws of natural language evolution; we can know how it functions in the communication and process it. The use of Old or Regional Romanian should not be judged as mistaken reporting them to the standard rules, but it is in accordance with other rules which we must discover.

Linguists are increasingly interested in the study of old languages with modern tools and their demand for old language processing tools is growing worldwide. Consequently, the computational linguists are building Diachronic and Old Corpora for all the natural languages, some described in many related works, as: Borin and Forsberg (2008), Davies (2010), Prevost and Stein (2013), etc.

We have built a sub-corpus for the Old Romanian, another for the regional variants, but it is more difficult to build corpora for the South Danube Romanian dialects (because they are very different from the standard language, cannot be understood by his speakers and two of them have no written aspect).

The emergence of South-Danube dialects is historically and politically determined. Due to their isolation of the linguistic center, they are more conservative than this one and retain many archaic linguistic phenomena.

Matteo Giulio Bartoli 1925 formulates the theory of isolated area or side areas, demonstrating with some examples that these areas are more conservative than the center. The dialects conserve more forms of the old languages or of the language where they were inherited (in our case, the Latin language).

For example, Istroromanian is the dialect of

the Romanian spoken by the smallest number of speakers, in eight villages in Croatia by 1,000 people, called "Vlach", only recently recognized as a national minority. This is an isolated area, very conservative for the Old Romanian. Through its disappearance and the lack of collected and digitized testimonies we could lose important data on the evolution of the Romanian language.

The dialectal variations study is important for the history of languages and for the etymology. The big etymological dictionary of Roman languages DeRom[1] has between its bibliographical sources books of specialists in dialectology as: Iosif Popovici 1909 and Richard Sarbu 1998 for the Istroromanian dialect.

Besides their historical importance, these dialects are languages of disadvantaged minorities, threatened with extinction, with limited access to culture. Their folk creation and other contributions must be conserved and the people speaking it have to be received into the family of European languages.

2 Related Work

The need for a research infrastructure for the study of historical lexical resources by digitization and implication of language technology is increasingly recognized by the historical research community. Historical documents are being digitized on a vast scale in cultural heritage and digital library projects in many countries. Modern linguistics studies pays increasing attention to diachronic and dialectal variations of languages. Similar corpora of other languages have started from contemporary language processing tools by adapting them to their old or regional variants.

Digitized historical corpora are already created for many languages: English Yanez-Bouza (2011), Davies (2012), Spanish and Portuguese Davies (2010), French Stein (2008) and so on. In another paper, France Martineau 2007 analyze the use of probabilistic parsing methods for old French texts. Unfortunately, the described probabilistic parser was trained and can be used only within the project and cannot be adapted for other language and annotation conventions.

Thus, Nuria Yanez-Bouza 2011 describes the building of a rule-based automate pre-annotator which has around 30 rules to identify complex verb forms (VCOMP), adjective phrases (AP), noun phrases (NP) and prepositional phrases (PP). The next phase is the manual annotation via a special interface. We also have a hybrid POS-tagger which permits the introduction of rules (see below) and use the manual annotation for a part of the semantic relations.

In another paper Borin et al. (2010) present an ongoing work on the building of digitalized diachronic Swedish lexical resource. The paper presents a basic research infrastructure for language technology called BLARK (Basic Language Resource Kit) which includes basic lexical resources, annotated corpora and basic NLP tools for processing these corpora. The same authors Borin and Forsberg (2008) describe the creation of the tool for the morphological analyze of Old Swedish words, which should be followed by syntactic and semantic analysis. East European languages have several preprocessing issues. For example, for some of them Cyrillic and Latin scripts were used in various periods of time; hence some documents need to be transliterated before further processing (Gruszczynski and Ogrodniczuk, 2015).

3 Tools for Romanian Standard Processing

3.1 The UAIC-Ro Hybrid Part Of Speech (POS)-Tagger

The tools for the processing of the Contemporary Romanian are the basis for creating the ones for the old or regional Romanian processing. The lexicon of the UAIC-POS-tagger for Contemporary Romanian also contains archaic words and forms, extracted from dictionaries, while Old Romanian also contains words and forms used today.

The UAIC-Ro POS-tagger is hybrid, i.e. successfully combines a statistical model with a rule based system (Simionescu, 2011). The specificity of the hybrid model is that it applies a set of rules to reduce the large set of valid pairs lemma and POS-tag (abbreviated morphological analysis) which can be applied at a word-form. In fact, there are morphological homonyms, interpretable taking into account the words in the vicinity of their occurrence. After the reduction of the set of possible analysis, the statistical system is put into operation.

The dictionary of the POS-tagger is formed of triplets: word-form, lemma (the basis form of word, found in dictionaries), POS-tag (an abbrevi-

[1] http://www.degruyter.com/view/product/205712

ated morphological analysis). The amount of the POS-tagger lexicon is related with the accuracy of the tool. The tool for the Contemporary Romanian contains 1,15 million distinct words extracted from dictionaries and 100,000 proper nouns extracted from Wikipedia. The set of 406 tags are a reduced version of the tagset used by the Multext East project Erjavec (2004).

The rule of big dimensions shows that the higher the number of tags is, the greater the gold corpus for the training must be. The training corpus for Contemporary Romanian consists in the NAACL 2003 corpus (39,000 sentences), and another 28,000 sentences extracted from the JRC-ACQUIS. The corpus for evaluation was Orwell's novel 1984, manually annotated in the Multext East project.

But these corpora were not have identical set of conventions and not use our tagset. The training corpus is not entirely manually corrected. It is possible that there are inconsistencies between the annotation of these corpora. The accuracy of the tool, evaluated on standard Romanian, is 95.12 % without rules and 96.66 % with rules.

The POS-tagger has been trained on standardized, but also on non-standardized language, before processing 2,570 sentences in Social Media communication (Romanian chat). A method to increase the accuracy on chat sentences was to double the training corpus, with and without letters with specific Romanian diacritics: ş, ă, ţ, î, â, that are not always used in chat communication.

For the diacritics only RO-POS tagger evaluated on Orwell's 1984 novel, we obtain an accuracy of 97.03 %. For the diacritics only RO-POS tagger, evaluated on the chat corpus the accuracy was only 68.67 %, for the Mixed diacritics RO-POS tagger, evaluated on mixed 1984, the accuracy was 94.38 %, and for the Mixed diacritics RO-POS tagger, evaluated on the chat corpus, the accuracy was 84.78 %, as shown in Perez 2016.

For difficult texts (old, non-standardized, new styles of communication not yet trained) we largely use manual validation of the output of the tool, and by the bootstrapping method, the corrected sentences are added to the gold training corpus.

3.2 The Malt Parser trained on Romanian

A variant of the Malt parser trained on UAIC-RoDepTb began to operate satisfactorily. The conventions of annotation used are in FDG (Functional Dependency Grammar), with labels of classical syntax, with numerous semantic subclassifications of modifiers. Creating the treebank in 2007, Augusto Perez had the intention of targeting the treebank for didactic purposes, for medium learning, even building a computer game to prepare students for exams, but, of course, the learning system cannot be so easily convinced to adopt the Dependency Grammar.

This system can be transposed both into the modern syntactic system of Universal Dependencies (UD) with loss of semantic information and into a semantic annotation system by adding information. This is why we will continue to use this classic format, in which the processing tools were trained, and then it will be automatically (supervised) converted into UD (Universal Dependencies) and into a semantic annotation.

The parser is named multilingual or universal in Hall et al. (2006), because its functioning is based only on dependency relations, on the training and on the morphological previously annotation in no matter what language. The accuracy of the parser is determined by the size of the training corpus, more than 10,000 sentences, by the exactitude of the morphological annotation, and by the consistency of the syntactic conventions. Thus, the syntactic parser will not cause problems if used for annotation of ancient or regional texts, respecting consistently the conventions of UAIC-RoDia Deptreebank, if the difficult problem of correct morphological annotation will be solved.

The parser was successfully used for syntactic annotation in the 2,570 chat phrases. On this occasion we found that the parser has a better accuracy after being trained on a large corpus which contains standard and non-standard sentences. After the training only with chat sentences, the accuracy on chat was 71.74 % for head attachment, 66.08 % for label attachment and 62.31 % for both attachment.

Using the same method, after the training with 15,000 sentences from all types of texts, including 4,000 sentences from the seventeenth century, and after the creation of Old Ro POS-tagger, the accuracy of our parser evaluated on Old Romanian was, for both attachments, 77.06 %, for head attachment, 83.79 %, and for label attachment, 82.5 %. The results are better than on chat corpus, because the training corpus was bigger, and we used the new Old Ro POS tagger (described below) with a satisfactory accuracy, with the output entirely manually corrected.

3.3 POS-tagger for the Old and Dialectal Romanian

For building a series of Old Romanian processing tools, we began by building a POS-tagger for Old Romanian, which would give us basic annotation for the syntactic and semantic parsers or for any other type of annotation. To build a new POS-tagger, a list of tags, a lexicon, and a training corpus is needed. After the elaboration of these data, we can make clones of the UAIC hybrid POS-tagger, described above, and of the POS-tagger of the Institute of Mathematics and Computer Science of Chisinau, Republic of Moldova, which can analyze also Romanian words written in Cyrillic letters.

3.3.1 The List of Tags for the Old Ro POS-tagger

To establish the list of tags for the new POS-tagger, we began with the list of the UAIC hybrid POS-tagger for Contemporary Romanian, reintroducing some tags which had been eliminated, i.e. the detailed analysis of personal and reflexive pronouns (dative and accusative case, strong and weak forms) and the complex tags for the relational words (prepositions, conjunctions, relative adverbs). The first category (personal and reflexive pronouns) is useful to differentiate the direct and indirect objects, to establish the co-references and the expletives.

A new set of tags which we introduced, original ones, were aimed at annotating language specific phenomenon of (Old) Romanian, namely the negation of non-personal synthetic modes (participle, gerund and supine) by the prefix ne-. Words as "*neterminat*","*nestricată*", "*neştiind*" (En: *unfinished, unbroken, not knowing*) have the lemma "*a termina*" (*to finish*), "*a strica*" (*to break*), "*a şti*" (*to know*), because the verbs "**a netermina*", "**a nestrica*", "**a neşti*" do not exist. The pos-tag of these forms will be annotated as: "*Vmp–sm-z*", "*Vmp–pf-z*", "*Vmg—–z*". (participle negative singular masculine, participle negative plural feminine, gerund negative). The opposite tag to "*Vmp–pf-z*" has, on the eighth position, the p that means "*positive*".

The annotation of verbal participles as adjectives is not acceptable, and has been corrected everywhere in the training corpus. We intend to build a dictionary of predicate arguments and adjunct structures (Cenel-Augusto Perez, 2015), and the participle has the same possible (syntactic and semantic) dependencies as the other verbal forms. We do not accept the letters y / n for annotating categories other than +/- definiteness, because they are not transparent and can be confusing, as shown in Mărănduc et al. (2016).

Finally, if the above forms are possible, but uncommon in Contemporary Romanian, there are tags needed to annotate specific forms only of the Old language. The list of tags for the forms of Dh (emphatic determiners) was also doubled as Ph (emphatic pronouns), because these forms exist in Old Romanian independently, not only as determiners of a noun. The emphatic adjective has a lot of specific forms in Old Romanian: "*eluşi*", "*eişi*", "*luişi*" (En: *himself, themselves*). Another phenomenon is the imperative formed from the long infinitive. Example: "*Nu vă teameţi!*" (with short infinitive) "*Nu vă teamereţi!*" (with long infinitive) (En: *Do not be afraid!*)

In Contemporary Romanian, the relative pronoun "*care*" has a very reduced inflection, and in Old Romanian the inflection is complex. Examples: "*carele*" *Pw3msry*, "*carea*" *Pw3fsry*, "*cari*" *Pw3mpr*, "*carii*" *Pw3mpry* (En: *which*).

The new tagset for the Old Romanian has 540 tags. All these tags was annotated in the entire corpus and the tags which do not exist in the tagset was eliminated from all the sub-corpora and from the lexicon of the POS-tagger. In this way we assured the consistency of the training corpus with the lexicon.

3.3.2 The Lexicon for the Old Ro POS-tagger

The collection of texts in Old Romanian is quite advanced; it contains 23 documents in TXT format from the sixteenth century, 60 from the seventeenth, 76 from the eighteenth and 325 from the nineteenth century. These texts were cleaned of the meta-text, specialists comments and notes, then processed by a concordancer program that builds indexes and makes statistics of the number of occurrences for each form in all the 500 books in text format opened. The concordancer used is the Lucon 03.16, the Cătălin Mititelu's program, available on Sourceforge site[2].

However, the old Romanian texts were written

[2]https://sourceforge.net/directory/os:windows/?q=Lucon

in Old Cyrillic letters. The collection that we hold contains both scans with Cyrillic and transcripts in Latin letters made by specialists. There was no Optical Character Recognizer (OCR) program for such letters. The letters differ from one book to another and there are many transitional alphabets with mixed Latin and Cyrillic letters. Our colleagues from the Institute of Mathematics and Computer Science of the Academy of Sciences of Moldova are now building an OCR which began operating satisfactorily for some texts (Cojocaru et al., 2017).

In the case of the Romanian language written with Cyrillic, we used the same lexicon for the Old-Romanian POS-tagger and for the OCR program, having two variants, with the word forms written in Latin letters and written in Cyrillic letters, trying to help our colleagues to increase the performances of the OCR for Romanian Cyrillic letters. The lexicon is obtained from the annotation of the Gospel, the first part of the New Testament (1648) having 5,028 sentences, text partially obtained by the cited above OCR program.

We have about 500 scanned old books without transcription in Latin alphabet. We hope that the new OCR will solve this problem. The solution of transcriptions made by specialists is questionable, because the specialists made sometimes interpretative transcriptions, closer to the old text, approaching it by the contemporary language (so that the POS-tagger will not recognize them in the text obtained by OCR) and introduced numerous notes and comments in contemporary language, while their elimination is time consuming.

Using the Lucon program, we created a lexicon to be introduced in the POS-tagger, with 120,000 word-forms. However, we do not know which number of actualized forms of words it contains; after the OCR processing of more printed old books, we will construct a more authentic lexicon.

Using the program DEPAR (Dictionary Parser) (Mărănduc et al., 2017) we extracted a list of 5,000 stable unanalyzable Multi Word Expressions from a dictionary (Mărănduc, 2010), and also 98,000 lexical or spelling variants extracted from the Thesaurus Dictionary[3]. The variants are generally old or regional, consequently their introduction in the POS-tagger lexicon is useful for the processing both of the Old and of the regional variants of the Daco-Romanian dialect (the name used by the dialectologists for the language spoken in Romania), but they are not useful for the South Danube dialects, that have special dictionaries.

The project Monumenta Linguae Dacoromanorum[4], started in 1988 in cooperation with the Freiburg University, has the purpose to digitize the old religious books in Romanian. A new edition of the first Bible printed in Romanian (1688) has been completed by using manually checked automatic morphologic annotation; we have received the indices of their edition, using another system of abbreviations compatible with ours, to be introduced in our Old Ro POS-tagger lexicon.

Finally, the result will be processed with a tool that generates complete paradigms of words (adding possible forms that do not appear in the indexed texts). We have such a tool for the Contemporary Romanian, called Anamorph (Timofciuc et al., 2013), and now a variant for Old Romanian has been built and its training must begin (Gîfu and Simionescu, 2016). All variants of the word are associated with the contemporary lemma, and the inflexion is generated starting from the root of the word form chosen in the text.

3.3.3 The training corpus for the Old Ro POS-tagger

The third step is the construction of a training corpus for the Old Romanian POS-tagger. We have no other solution than to train the POS-tagger and the Malt parser on the contemporary gold corpus, then to process the old texts, and then to correct the output of the tools, at the beginning having a modest accuracy.

The manually corrected sentences will form in time the training corpus for the Old Romanian. The module attached of the POS-tagger will extract from these manually corrected annotations the forms or the analysis that does not exist in its lexicon and will add them. An increase of the accuracy of the POS-tagger is expected after the increasing of the training corpus, i. e. after the manually correction of more books automatically annotated with this tool. The training corpus (having now 18,187 sentences, including 6,882 of the 17th to 19th centuries) is smaller than the one for the Standard Romanian POS-tagger, but is consistent with the tagset. The POS-tagger for the Old Romanian has now an accuracy of 91.66 %.

[3]http://edtlr.info.uaic.ro/

[4]https://consilr.info.uaic.ro/ mld/monumenta/

3.3.4 Building POS-taggers for processing the South Danube Dialects

Then, we will apply the same solution: to build a few clones of the UAIC-Ro-POS-tagger for each South-Danube dialect. The same steps must be completed for each South-Danube dialect, beginning with the difficult step of the acquisition of digitized sources.

The construction of the Regional lexicon begins with the acquisition of a big collection of sources: texts in each variant of the language, in editable form. Then, two problems must be solved: first, it needs a big lexicon containing all the possible word-forms in each dialect of the language, with the lemmas and with the correct morphological analysis for any form find in texts, and secondly, it needs a big gold corpus (manually checked) for the training.

The greater difficulty lies in the fact that there is a very big distance between these variants of the language, we will need to start from zero the construction of the training corpus for each dialect, without using the large corpus of the other variants of the language. It can only be used as training corpus on regional variants spoken in Romania and the Republic of Moldova

We have a collection of texts published by specialists from each dialect and some dictionaries. In order to create a collection of sources, we should do dialectal surveys in the villages where the dialects are spoken, because two of them do not have a written aspect, to register and annotate the texts. We have not yet a collection of annotated specimens of Spontaneous spoken language in our corpus.

We can extract lemmas from the dictionaries using the program DEPAR (Dictionary Parser) (Mărănduc et al., 2017), but the inflexion must be manually introduced in the POS-tagger lexicon. For this purpose, we will have to associate specialists in the South-Danube dialects in our project. The existence of a lexicon with flexionary forms could also lead to the creation of OCR for the Aromanian dialect, that has a written aspect. The difficulty is that various phonetic transcription systems are used in different published collections.

Figure 1: The map of Aromanians localities, from the http://www.theapricity.com/forum/showthread

4 Short Presentation of Romanian Dialects

4.1 The Aromanian Dialect

Aromanian is the dialect with the most speakers, approximately 250,000. They live in Albania, in Greece, (the Pindos Mountains, the province of Macedonia) or in the Republic of Macedonia, hence the name of the Macedo dialect, that can be confusing, because this is the name of a geographical region, and in that region there are also people of other origins and languages.

There are numerous texts in this dialect, because more people speaking it migrated in Romania and ones of them become specialists in dialectal linguistics. For example, Marioţeanu (2006), Saramandu (2003) and Nevaci (2011), for mentioning only the contemporary ones. Other older collections are Capidan (1925), Obedenaru and Bianu (1891), Bujduveanu (2005), and so on. They have published collections of texts in more styles of the language, written or oral popular literature, dictionaries, textbooks. This dialect has been studied from the nineteen century and it has historical variants (texts in Old Aromanian). It has also different regional variants. (see Figure 1)

However, there are several difficulties. The pronunciation is differently transcribed in different books, depending on the period in which they were collected and published. This dialect is also studied by the Greek linguists that have another set of graphical conventions for the transcription. The spelling interpretive conception, nearby the standard language, exists also on these specialists, also the intention to approach the Aromanian dialect to the standard language exists, especially since it is the only one who enjoys the existence of schools and manuals in the Aromanian.

Aromanian is no option in any OCR software, neither in the automated programs for the translation, and various letters with diacritics are not recognized. For the moment, the editable text obtained by OCR is of poor quality and should be carefully corrected by specialists in South-Danube Romanian dialects. Probably we have to introduce the three South-Danube dialects as independent options in the OCR program, each with its lexicon, including the letters from all the transcription systems.

4.2 The Meglenoromanian Dialect

The Meglenoromanians are an ethnic group living in the Meglen region of Central Macedonia, Greece. This ethnic group is less numerous than the Aromanians. The researchers estimated their number at 20,000 persons in the nineteenth century. However, Thede Kahl 2006 estimated them at 5,000 persons; the negative demographic dynamic is evident. The minorities are not recognized in Greece, and in Turkey they are submitted at an assimilation and islamization process. There are no schools in the Meglenoromanian dialect. This idiom, having no written aspect, has no cult literature. However, literary folklore texts were published by many linguists. More collections were published by Pericles Papahagi 1902, Ion Aurel Candrea 1925a, 1925b, and Theodor Capidan 1925. There is only one cult publication, a brochure about silkworm rearing with the script adapted, and terms borrowed from Romanian. The Megleno idiom is endangered, it was entered in the UNESCO Red Book on endangered languages, the "Languages in grave danger" and UNESCO Atlas of Languages in danger in the world. (Atanasov, 2014). Unlike the Aromanians, who are mostly herdsmen, the Meglenoromanians are traditionally occupied by agriculture. They are not nomads, but sedentary and therefore this dialect suffered fewer external influences and was kept as a native language spoken in the family. In the Figure 2 there is a map of their localities, extract from the Th. Capidan study, 1928. More families emigrated in the Dobrudja region of Romania. (see Figure 2).

Therefore, we have to contribute to the preservation of texts in the Meglenoromanian dialect, and to facilitate the access of the European culture for this disfavored linguistic community, by

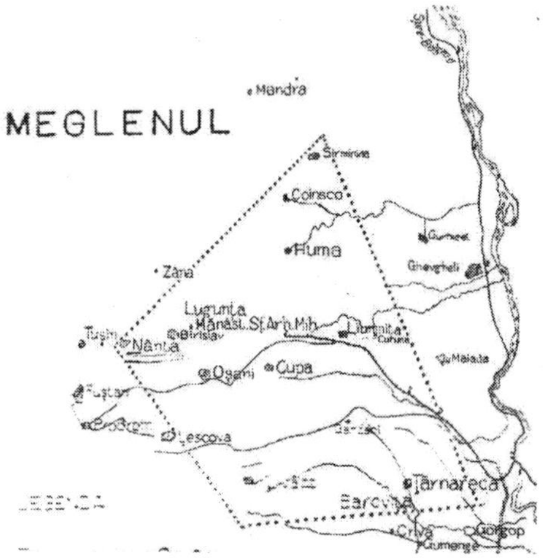

Figure 2: The map of Meglenoromanians localities, drew by T. Capidan

building an annotated corpus for this idiom and by computerizing their dialect. A computerized form of their dictionaries and lexicons is also necessary. The annotated corpus and the electronic dictionary will be used to build a machine translation.

4.3 Short Presentation of the Istroromanian Dialect

Istroromanian is an Eastern Romance idiom spoken in a few villages in the peninsula of Istria, in Croatia. The number of Istroromanian speakers is more than 500, the "smallest ethnic group in Europe". In the eighteen century the number of speakers was 10,000, and many toponyms with origin in Istroromanian dialect demonstrate this fact. Part of speakers are migrants in Europe, USA, Canada or Australia.

It is listed among languages that are "seriously endangered" in the UNESCO Red Book of Endangered Languages. Since 2010, the Croatian Constitution recognizes Istroromanians as one of 22 national minorities. However, there have not been significant changes in preserving their language, culture and ethnic identity. (see Figure 3).

Given the fact that Istroromanians have long been in a gradual process of assimilation, and their language was not used in writing, it is strongly influenced by the Croatian language, and there are no documents to be processed, except a small number of texts collected by linguists: Feresini (1996), Pușcariu (1906), Cantemir (1959). Currently there are some rescue actions for the preservation of Istroromanian language, carried out by cultural associations.

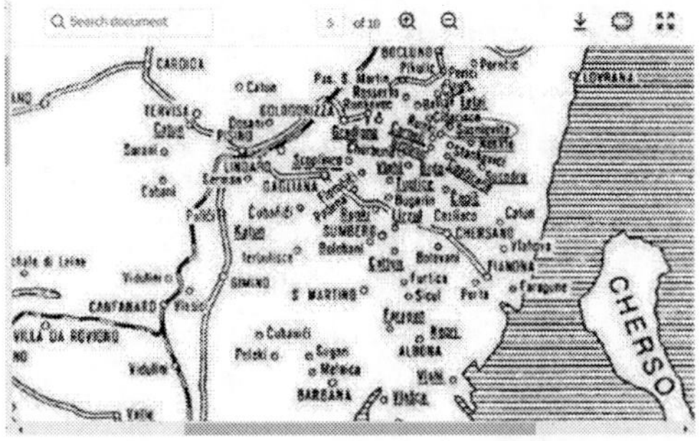

Figure 3: The map of Istroromanians localities, drew by Pericle Papahagi

A digitization of all the published texts in Istroromanian and their carefully annotation is necessary. There are some lexicons to be computerized and linked to the dictionaries of the other South-Danube dialects and to the Romanian computerized dictionaries. In the table 1, some differences between the Romanian dialects are exemplified. We ignored here the different diacritics of letters.

5 Discussion

5.1 The Linguistic Correct Definition of the Variants of the Romanian

The linguistic definition for the concept of dialect is that this variant of the language is quite different from the language standard, and mutual understanding between the speakers of the dialect and the speakers of the standard language is quite difficult or even impossible. In cases where differences are small and the understanding between speakers is easy, these are not different dialects, but simple regional variants. Such is the case of the language spoken in the Republic of Moldova, sometimes referred to as an independent language, or as a different dialect of the Romanian, for no linguistic reasons. However, to demonstrate this truth we need big corpora in the language spoken in the Republic of Moldova and in the South-Danube dialects, all morphologically and syntactically annotated, and then we can statistically calculate the indices of the approach or departure from the standard Romanian of each of these idioms. The creation of a big Romanian corpus with morphological and syntactic annotations, illustrating all the geographical and historical variations of this language is a long time project, which will continue probably since 2020 or more years. The corpus had counted in 2014 only 4,600 sentences in Romanian Standard (Perez, 2014).

5.2 Aromanian: A Dialect or an Independent Idiom?

We can establish with scientific arguments if this dialect has the tendency to become an independent natural language or to remain a dialect of Romanian, without imposing any solution, but only to ascertain if, as some experts have said, Aromanian is a language independent appertaining of the group of Romance languages.

The national consciousness of speakers, resulting on their texts, is also important for establish whether it's an independent idiom. Aromanians are divided into three main groups: the first, living in northern and central Greek Macedonia, called Gramushtenians, the second living in the Pindos mountains, called Pindenians, the third living in the south of Epirus, and in Thessaly, called Farsherots. However, the speakers of this dialect have different conceptions about their nationality. According with the testimonies of early researchers, the first two groups consider that they are Aromanians, but the Farsherots consider that they are Romanians. By studying texts collected more soon we will see if these conceptions of Aromanians about themselves were kept or changed.

6 Future Work

The corpus which we intend to create can be useful to create computerized dictionaries for the Romanian dialects aligned with those of standard Romanian language (and of Romanian Word Net (RoWN), aligned at Princeton Word Net (PWN), and to build a machine translation system for these isolated idioms, to introduce them in the international circulation. The cultural and linguistic isolation of these speakers will cease, if a platform, such as Babel, will be able to translate into these dialects the information that the speakers find on the Internet in a well-known language.

6.1 Study of the Historical Variations and of the Evolution Tendencies

Another important utility of the corpus that we begin building now is the statistic demonstration of the evolution tendencies. The Aromanian is the most important dialect of the Romanian after the standard language, called the Dacoromanian dialect. The comparative study of Aromanian texts from different historical periods with statistical methods will allow us to know what is their evolution tendency, whether the trend of this idiom

Istro-Romanian	Aromanian	Megleno-Romanian	Romanian	English
klieptu	cheptu	klieptu	piept	chest
bire	ghine	bini	bine	well, good
bliera	azghirari	zber	zbiera	to roar
filiu	hilj	iliu	fiu	son
filia	hilje	ilie	fiică	daughter
flier	heru	ieru	fier	iron
viţelu	yiţal	viţal	viţel	calf
(g)lierm	iermu	ghiarmi	vierme	worm

Table 1: Differences between few words in the Romanian Dialects

is approaching the Romanian standard language or the Greek language, whether it becomes an independent idiom or not. We plan to compare parts of our corpora using various comparison methods in order to better understand their similarities and dissimilarities.

7 Conclusions

In this paper we described an ongoing work on the creation of a big balanced corpus of Old and Regional Romanian texts, impossible without creating tools for its processing. Consequently, we described some such as tools used for the development of our corpus in several directions.

The balanced corpus does not have only a scientific interest, but also practical consequences. If the language spoken in the Republic of Moldova is easily understandable by Romanian speakers without consulting a bilingual dictionary, it demonstrates that the Moldavian is not a dialect of Romanian. However, in the case of South-Danube dialects, there are dictionaries and also final lexicons in the published books, that being necessary in order to allow Romanian readers to understand the published texts. That is proof that they are dialects and there cannot be any mutual understanding between their speakers.

References

1902. *Meglenoromanians. Folk Ethnographic Study.* Socec & Co publisher, Bucharest.

Peter Atanasov. 2014. The current state of megleno-romanians. megleno-romanian, an endangered idiom. *Memoria Ethnologica* XIV(52-53):3037.

Matteo Bartoli. 1925. *Introduzione alla neolinguistica: (princìpi-scopi-metodi).* 2. Biblioteca dell' Archivum Romanicum - Serie II: Linguistica. `https://books.google.ro/books?id=Zg0MAAAAIAAJ`.

Lars Borin, Marcus Forsberg, and Dimitrios Kokkinakis. 2010. Diabase: Towards a diachronic blark in support of historical studies. In *Proceedings of LREC.*. pages 35–42.

Lars Borin and Markus Forsberg. 2008. Something old, something new: A computational morphological description of old swedish. In *LREC 2008 - Workshop on Language Technology for Cultural Heritage Data (LaTeCH 2008) Conference Proceedings*. pages 9–16.

Tănase Bujduveanu. 2005. *The Sărăcăcians.* Aromanian Book Publisher, Reading, Massachusetts.

Ion Aurel Candrea. 1925a. Meglenoromanian texts. *Speech and Soul* I/I:261285.

Ion Aurel Candrea. 1925b. Meglenoromanian texts. *Speech and Soul* I/II:100128.

Traian Cantemir. 1959. *Istroromanian Texts.* Romanian Academy Publisher, Institute of Linguistics Cluj.

Theodor Capidan. 1925. *Meglenoromanians. Their History and Their Language.* National Culture / Romanian Academy, Bucharest.

Theodor Capidan. 1928. *The Meglenoromanians. Their Folk Literature.* Socec & Co publisher, Bucharest.

Cătălina Mărănduc Radu Simionescu Cenel-Augusto Perez. 2015. Ro-paas a resource linked to our uaic-ro-dep-treebank. In *Advances in Artificial Intelligence and Soft Computing 14th Mexican International Conference on Artificial Intelligence, MICAI 2015*. pages 29–46.

Cătălina Mărănduc Radu Simionescu Cenel-Augusto Perez. 2016. Social media processing romanian chats and discourse analysis. *Computacin y Sistemas* 20(3):404–414.

Svetlana Cojocaru, Alexander Colesnicov, and Ludmila Malahova. 2017. Digitization of old romanian texts printed in the cyrillic script. In *Proceedings of International Conference on Digital Access to Textual Cultural Heritage*. pages 143–148.

Mark Davies. 2010. Creating useful historical corpora: A comparison of corde, the corpus del espanol, and the corpus do português pages 137–166.

Mark Davies. 2012. Expanding horizons in historical linguistics with the 400 million word corpus of historical american english. *Corpora* (7):121–157.

Tomaz Erjavec. 2004. Multext-east version 3: Multilingual morphosyntactic specifications, lexicons and corpora. In *Proceedings of the Fourth Conference on Language Resources and Evaluation, LREC2004*. `http://nl.ijs.si/ME/`.

Nerina Feresini. 1996. *Il Comune Istro-romeno di Valdarsa*. Edizioni Italo Svevo, Trieste.

Daniela Gîfu and Radu Simionescu. 2016. Tracing language variation for romanian. In *Proceedings of the 17th International Conference on Intelligent Text Processing and Computational Linguistics, CICLing*.

Wlodzimierz Gruszczynski and Maciej Ogrodniczuk. 2015. The electronic corpus of the 17th and 18th century polish texts (up to 1772) aims, methods, current state, problems and prospects for development. In *Slavic Corpus Linguistics: The Historical Dimension*. pages 21–25.

Johan Hall, Joakim Nivre, and Jens Nilsson. 2006. Discriminative classifiers for deterministic dependency parsing. In *Proceedings of the 21st International Conference on Computational Linguistics and 44th Annual Meeting of the Association for Computational Linguistics (COLING-ACL)*. pages 316–323.

Thede Kahl. 2006. The islamisation of the meglen vlachs (megleno-romanians): The village of nânti (nótia) and the nântinets in present-day turkey. *Nationalities Papers* 34(1):71–90. https://doi.org/10.1080/00905990500504871.

Cătălina Mărănduc. 2010. *The Dictionary of Romanian Expressions, Syntagms and Phrases (DELS)*. Corint Publishing, Bucharest.

Cătălina Mărănduc, Ludmila Malahov, Cenel-Augusto Perez, and Alexandru Colesnicov. 2016. Rodia project of a regional and historical corpus for romanian. In *Proceedings of MFOI*. pages 268–284.

Cătălina Mărănduc, Cătălin Mititelu, and Radu Simionescu. 2017. Parsing romanian specialized dictionaries structured in nests. In *Proceedings of Digital Access to Textual Cultural Heritage (DATeCH)*. pages 35–41.

Matilda Caragiu Marioţeanu. 2006. *Aromanians and Aromanian Dialect in Contemporary Consciousness*. Romanian Academy Publisher, Bucharest.

France Martineau, Constana Rodica Diaconescu, , and Paul Hirschbühler. 2007. Le corpus voies du francais : de lelaboration à lannotation pages 121–142.

Manuela Nevaci. 2011. *The Gray of the Frontier Aromanians in Dobrogea*. Cartea Universitară Publishing House, Bucharest.

Gheorghiad Mihail Obedenaru and Ioan Bianu. 1891. *Macedoromanans Texts. Fairy Tales and Folk Poems from Crushova*. Carol Göbl Publisher, Bucharest.

Cenel-Augusto Perez. 2014. *Linguistic Resources for Natural Language Processing. (PhD thesis)*. Al. I. Cuza University, Iaşi.

Iosif Popovici. 1909. *The Romanian Dialects in Istria*. Halle.

Sophie Prevost and Achim Stein. 2013. *Syntactic Reference Corpus of Medieval French (SRCMF)*. ENS de Lyon; Universitt Stuttgart; Lattice, Lyon/Stuttgart/Paris.

Sextil Puşcariu. 1906. Istroromanian studies. in collaboration with m. bartoli, a. belulovici and a. byhan, vol. i. texts. *Romanian Academy Annals* series II,(tom. XXVIII):117–182.

Nicolae Saramandu. 2003. *Aromanian and Meglenoromanian Studies*. Ex Ponto Publisher, Constanţa.

Richard Sârbu and Vasile Frăţilă. 1998. *Istroromanan Dialect. Texts and Glossary*. Amarcord publisher, Timişoara.

Radu Simionescu. 2011. Hybrid pos tagger. *Proceedings of Language Resources and Tools with Industrial Applications Workshop Eurolan 2011 Summer school* .

Achim Stein. 2008. Syntactic annotation of old french text corpora. *Corpus* (7):157–172.

Ana Maria Timofciuc, Daniela Gîfu, and Corina Forăscu. 2013. A simple reliable web application for public discourse analysis. In *Proceedings of the International Conference on Intelligent Information Systems (IIS)*. pages 158–162.

Nuria Yanez-Bouza. 2011. Archer past and present (1990-2010). *ICAME Journal* (35):205–236.

Multilingual Ontologies for the Representation and Processing of Folktales

Thierry Declerck

DFKI GmbH,
Multilingual Technologies
Stuhlsatzenhausweg 3
D-66123 Saarbrücken
declerck@dfki.de

Anastasija Aman, Martin Banzer, Dominik Macháček, Lisa Schäfer, Natalia Skachkova
Saarland University
Computational Linguistics Department
P.O. Box 15 11 50
D-66041 Saarbrücken, Germany

Abstract

We describe work done in the field of folkloristics and consisting in creating ontologies based on well-established studies proposed by "classical" folklorists. This work is supporting the availability of a huge amount of digital and structured knowledge on folktales to digital humanists. The ontological encoding of past and current motif-indexation and classification systems for folktales was in the first step limited to English language data. This led us to focus on making those newly generated formal knowledge sources available in a few more languages, like German, Russian and Bulgarian. We stress the importance of achieving this multilingual extension of our ontologies at a larger scale, in order for example to support the automated analysis and classification of such narratives in a large variety of languages, as those are getting more and more accessible on the Web.

1 Introduction

A final goal of our work is to make high quality content in the larger field of folkloristics available to a broad range of applications involving language technologies. The content, which is based on well-established and widely used classical motif-indexation, description and classification systems for folklore and related narratives, has been ported to standard W3C[1] formal representation languages, like OWL[2], RDF(s)[3] and RDF[4].

The result of this work is an integrated ontology containing about 60,000 classes and instances that are interlinked and searchable by means of semantic query engines. The integrated ontology, encoding distinct types of descriptives for folktales, offers a unique combination of generic classifications of narrative types and very fine-grained motifs (or patterns) occurring in tales.

This ontology can be optimally re-used in the context of narrative engines supporting the re-organization and adaptation of plots and characters in different and new contexts of narration to be displayed in various environments, like automated text generation or audio story telling.

The original folktale knowledge sources that are now available in this rich semantic environment are the Thompson's Motif-Index of Folk-Literature (Thompson, 1955-1958), the Aarne-Thompson-Uther Classification System of International Folktales (Uther, 2004), the so-called Proppian functions and also the typical characters of (Russian) folktales (Propp, 1968).

The work by Propp is very relevant, as his approach was aiming not only at characterizing the elements of a tale, but also and mainly at describing the organization of such elements in a tale for building consistent stories. The influence

[1] https://www.w3.org/
[2] https://www.w3.org/OWL/
[3] https://www.w3.org/TR/rdf-schema/
[4] https://www.w3.org/RDF/

Proceedings of the LT4DHCSEE in conjunction with RANLP 2017, pages 20–23,
Varna, Bulgaria, 8 September 2017.

of the Proppian approach on the production of cinematic narratives has been studied and discussed in many publications (see for example (Fell, 1997)).

The ontologization of the Proppian elements, in combination with the Motifs Index and the Tales Types offers a very closely woven set of fined-grained modules that can serve as an (extensible) catalogue of basic plot elements. Instances for the Aarne-Thompson-Uther Classification System of International Folktales have been collected from various Web resources, like the ``Multilingual Folk Tale Database[5] and the "Ashliman collection"[6], so that we have now more than 4,000 stories included as instances in the ontology.

2 Towards Multilingual Ontologies for Folktales

In a first step we created an ontology based on one story, the Russian tale "Гуси-лебеди" (*The Magic Swan Geese*), including a large family ontology, as families are playing an important role in many tales. The ontology is described in (Koleva et al., 2012). This was our first development of a multilingual ontology in the field of folktales. Languages covered were English, German, Russian and Bulgarian.

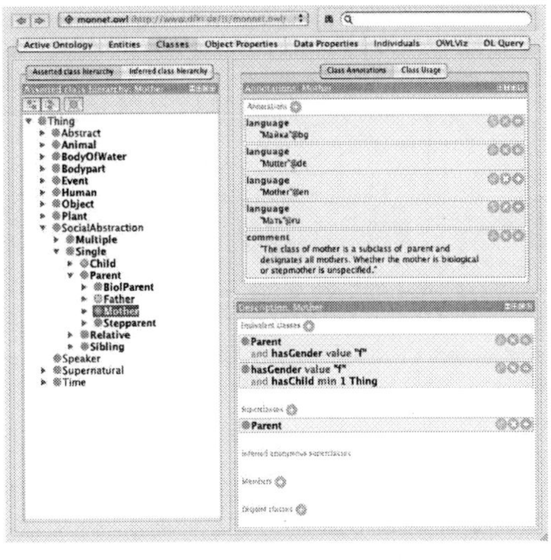

Figure 1: Screenshot from the Protégé tools, showing an element of the multilingual family class hierarchy in our first multilingual folktale ontology.

[5] http://www.mftd.org/index.php?action=atu

[6] http://www.pitt.edu/~dash/folktexts.html

In a second step, we proposed a multilingual ontologization of the Proppian system. A version is available now for English, German and Russian. This work was done together with 2 Russian native speakers, who could read the original version of the work by Propp, and could also extract the relevant terms from the German translation (published in 1972) and from the English version (Propp, 1968).

Table 1 gives an example on the way this multilingual information is encoded in our ontology, for the Proppian function "Interdiction".

```
:Gamma\~Interdiction
  rdf:type owl:Class ;
  rdf:type owl:NamedIndividual ;
  rdf:type
    SoPro:Instances-Propp-Function ;
  rdfs:comment "Dem Helden wird ein
    Verbot erteilt."@de ;
  rdfs:label "interdiction"@en ;
  rdfs:comment "An interdiction is
    addressed to the hero."@en ;
  rdfs:label "словозапрет"@ru ;
  rdfs:comment "К герою обращаются с
    запретом."@ru ;
  rdfs:label "Verbot"@de .
  SoPro:inHierarchyProppFunctionOf
    SoPro:Gamma1 ;
  SoPro:inHierarchyProppFunctionOf
    SoPro:Gamma2 ;
  rdfs:subClassOf
    SoPro:Propp-Function ;
.
```

Table 1: The Propp Function "Interdiction" in the ontology, including multilingual rdf(s) "label" and "comment" properties.

In Table 1, the reader can see how we encode the multilingual data using the RDF(s) annotation properties "label" and "comment". The texts encoded by those properties are taken directly from the Russian text and its official translations in English and German.

In a following step, we will provide for a translation of our ontology version of the Aarne-Thompson-Uther Classification System of International Folktales[7]. For adding German terms and descriptions of tale types we will use (Uther,

[7] See (Declerck et. al., 2017) for details on this ontology.

2015), a classification system for German folktale types covering to a great extent (Uther, 2004), but with German language data. Figure 2[8] is giving an idea of the type of hierarchical structure we are dealing with in this resource, which we abbreviate to "ATU".

- ANIMAL TALES 1-299
    - Wild Animals 1-99
        - The Clever Fox (Other Animal) 1-69
        - Other Wild Animals 70-99
    - Wild Animals and Domestic Animals 100-149
    - Wild Animals and Humans 150-199
    - Domestic Animals 200-219
    - Other Animals and Objects 220-299
- TALES OF MAGIC 300-749
    - Supernatural Adversaries 300-399
    - Supernatural or Enchanted Wife (Husband) or Other Relative 400-459
        - Wife 400-424
        - Husband 425-449
        - Brother or Sister 450-459
    - Supernatural Tasks 460-499
    - Supernatural Helpers 500-559
    - Magic Objects 560-649
    - Supernatural Power or Knowledge 650-699
    - Other Tales of the Supernatural 700-749

Figure 2: Example of the classification levels of ATU. ANIMAL TALES and TALES OF MAGIC are in the first level, Wild Animals, Wild Animals and Domestic Animals and Wild Animals and Humans are on the second level and The Clever Fox and Other Wild Animals are on the third level. The ranges behind each line are the so called ATU numbers which belong to each class.

A way to start to expand the language coverage of the ontological ATU resource lies for example in taking term equivalents that are available in corresponding Wikipedia articles, but this is limited by now to French, Estonian, Spanish, Hebrew, Chinese and Portuguese, which are the Wikipedia articles that contain a relevant number of ATU types in their language. There is a need thus to identify textual resources in other languages that are covering the ATU types.

The same strategy can be followed for obtaining the term equivalents for the Proppian functions and characters. We notice for example that the 31 function names are available in the Croatian Wikipedia article on Propp. Also the work (Propp, 1968) has been translated in the Bosnian-Croatian-Montenegrin-Serbian language (in 1982). And as (Propp, 1968) has been translated in quite some languages, it should be easy to extract from those translations the list of function and character terms.

3 Multilingual Folktale Resources

One goal of having different indexation, classification or other schemes for folktales standardized in one formal representation is to support NLP tasks applied to such types of texts and to allow their automated mark-up or classification along the lines of a well-established knowledge source.

There is one very interesting resource on the Web, called "Multilingual Folk Tale Database"[9], which is offering for some of the uploaded tale texts, in many languages, a corresponding type number from the Aarne-Thompson-Uther classification. The "Multilingual Folk Tale Database" is also displaying some folktales in a parallel fashion, in various languages, offering to a certain extent a comparable multilingual corpus of folktales.

This data can thus provide for a kind of gold standard for classification tasks, at least for tales in English, which are in the majority in the database. We wrote a crawler for accessing the content of the Multilingual Folktale Database and extracted folktales with available metadata. This gave us an access to information about the language, the ATU class number and its label.

4 Issues for a multilingual Classification Task

The Multilingual Folk Tale Database contains stories in 11 languages. We crawled all of them. Figure 3 summarizes the number of stories by language. In total we have 901 stories in English and between roughly 500 and 600 stories in other 4 languages, French, Spanish, Hungarian and Russian[10]. We realized that we have too few stories in German, Danish, Polish, Italian, Czech and Dutch to implement a strong supervised classifier for them. We also realized that many of the stories in the Multilingual Folk Tale Database do not have an ATU number assigned.

[8] Image taken from http://www.mftd.org/index.php?action=atu

[9] See again: http://www.mftd.org/index.php?action=atu

[10] Those figures are valid for May 2017, when we crawled the database.

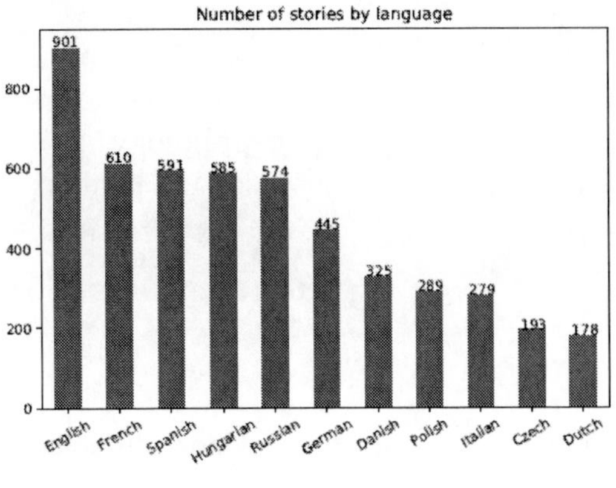

Figure 3: Number of all stories in the Multilingual Folk Tale Database by language (May 2017)

Figure 4 shows the numbers of stories with assigned ATU level 1 labels, for each language. The language with most labelled stories is English, with 342 labelled stories. The second is German, with 227 stories. For other languages we have too few resources. So there is a need to expand this kind of resources with tales from the corresponding languages.

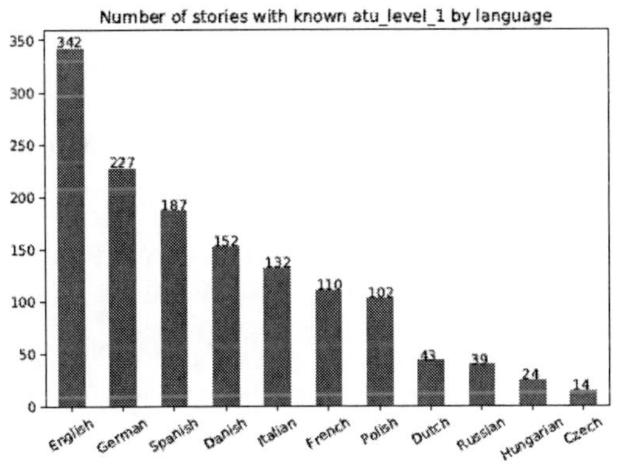

Figure 4: Number of stories in the Multilingual Folk Tale Database with an ATU type tag of level 1 by language (May 2017)

As the database of multilingual folktales is in continuous expansion, we are quite confident that in a limited amount of time a collection of tales in the languages of concerns for the LTDHCSEE workshop can be reached, whereas additional focus should be given on the correct assignment of ATU types to each tales.

5 Conclusions

In this short paper, we presented work done in generating multilingual ontologies that are encoding past and current "classical" (meaning non-digital-born) knowledge sources in the field of folklore, more specifically folktales. We described the current level of multilingualism in some of the ontologies we developed and proposed a way to extend this to more languages. Additionally we described a multilingual source of tales, which are partly labelled with the type numbers of the Aarne-Thompson-Uther classification scheme, and which can be used by now for an automated classification task for English folktales. We note that the current collection of labelled tales in other languages has to be considerably extended for allowing supervised training.

Acknowledgments

We thank the anonymous reviewers for their comments.

References

Thierry Declerck, Antónia Kostová and Lisa Schäfer. 2017. Towards a Linked Data Access to Folktales classified by Thompson's Motifs and Aarne-Thompson-Uther's Types. Proceedings of Digital Humanities 2017. Montréal.

John L. Fell. 1977. Vladimir Propp in Hollywood.Film Quarterly 30(3):19–28. https://doi.org/10.2307/1211770.

Nikolina Koleva, Thierry Declerck, and Hans-Ulrich Krieger. 2012. An ontology-based iterative text processing strategy for detecting and recognizing characters in folktales. In Jan Christoph Meister, editor, Digital Humanities 2012 Conference Abstracts, Hamburg University Press.

Vladimir Propp. 1968. Morphology of the folktale. Trans., Laurence Scott. 2nd ed., University of Texas Press.

Stith Thompson. 1955-1958. Motif-index of folk-literature: A classification of narrative elements in folktales, ballads, myths, fables, medieval romances, exempla,fabliaux, jest-books, and local legends. Revised and enlarged edition, Indiana University Press.

Hans-Jörg Uther. 2004. The Types of International Folktales: A Classification and Bibliography. Based on the system of Antti Aarne and Stith Thompson.Suomalainen Tiedeakatemia.

On the annotation of vague expressions: a case study on Romanian historical texts

Anca Dinu
Center for Digital Humanities
University of Bucharest
anca_d_dinu@yahoo.com

Walther v. Hahn,
Research Group "Computerphilology"
University of Hamburg
vhahn@informatik.uni-hamburg.de

Cristina Vertan,
Research Group "Computerphilology"
University of Hamburg
Cristina.vertan@uni-hamburg.de

Abstract

Current approaches in Digital .Humanities tend to ignore a central aspect of any hermeneutic introspection: the intrinsic vagueness of analyzed texts. Especially when dealing with historical documents neglecting vagueness has important implications on the interpretation of the results. In this paper we present current limitation of annotation approaches and describe a current methodology for annotating vagueness for historical Romanian texts.

1 Introduction

Digital Humanities (henceforth „DH") nowadays tend to use huge corpora („big data") to achieve reliable results with computer-based technologies. However, behind all interpretations, such as reliability discussions, stands a hermeneutic approach, which is always qualitative in nature. Such research can be backed up by quantitative descriptions of the material, which is basically the classical annotation method in DH. The scientific use of annotations is usually a positive ascription of features, such as „is reliable" or „is not reliable" and a statistics of the corresponding feature. This kind of approach ignores a fundamental aspect of the data, the vagueness of many assertions and thus the drawbacks of such crisp choice "is/is not".

In this article we describe recent on-going research activities in which we investigate to which extent assertions found in historical texts original texts or in their translations are:

- consistent within the same text and across the originals;
- reliable with respect to author's annotations or the annotations of further translators;
- consistent and reliable across different language versions.

We propose to support the hermeneutic traditional approach through the following computer-based methods:

1. an annotation formalism which allows the mark-up of different types of vagueness and its source;
2. a set of inference rules for the combination of such vague features to calculate an overall result of their reliability;
3. a similarity measurement of the inferred results obtained for the same queries on different translations.

2 Vaguenss theoretical an practical considerations in DH-projects

2.1 Theoretical approaches to vagueness in natural language.

Since a long time vagueness is described in theory (for German: Pinkal 1980) and processed in various conceptual and technical environments (Zadeh 1965). Data in humanities (history, arts, literature, music etc.) are subject to interpretation of the researcher and therefore their possible or real vagueness must be kept for final resolution.

In historical texts - more than in modern texts - many vague expressions are standard for describing events, attitudes or even factual data (v.Hahn 2015). Writing them into a standard data base would distort the entries, because its later processing in inferences will treat them as true facts.

Indefiniteness (Unbestimmtheit) is a central feature of natural language. Any type of text (even the very specialised ones (v. Hahn, 1983)) includes indefinite expressions. According to Pinkal (Pinkal

Proceedings of the LT4DHCSEE in conjunction with RANLP 2017, pages 24–31,
Varna, Bulgaria, 8 September 2017.

1980), (Pinkal 1985) one can evaluate the degree of indefiniteness ("Unbestimmtheit") in an expression according to three criteria

4. Semantic vagueness
5. Unclearness of the illocutive role
6. 3 the communicative expression can be unclear, when from the point of view of the situation and the recipient it is too less informative

An expression is indefinite when only by means of imposing other conditions one can assign to it the value "true" or "false". Such conditions can have a semantic or pragmatic nature. We will refer here strictly at the semantic nature. According to Pinkal, the semantic indefiniteness can be either vague or ambiguous. Vagueness has several sources: either porosity of language or imprecision at expression's borders, inexactity, one or multidimensional relativeness. Ambiguity is due to several natural language features like: Homonymy, polysemy, syntactical ambiguity, multiple referential meaning, and dual metaphorical meaning

Vagueness is related more to the conceptual backbone of the language, while ambiguity relates to words and terms. Vagueness can be preserves across languages, while ambiguity can be present in just one language.

Computer linguistics concentrates often more on ambiguity, by means of resources like Wordnet[1]. Vagueness detection is in strict correlation with conceptual modelling of the text. In the current proposal we will investigate to which extent vagueness influence the hermeneutic interpretation of historical sources. However translation can be often of source of transforming ambiguous expression in source language in vague expressions in the target language, especially if the knowledge base is reduced and the source and the target language belong to different language families.

2.2 Computer-based approaches for historical document analysis

Processing multilingual (historical) texts beyond digital reproduction of paper versions, implies several obligatory steps:

Definition and formal representation of concepts which are relevant for the document(s);

Annotation of these concepts within the documents also by means of automatic processes implying text minning and natural language processing (named entity recognition, lemmatization, PoS tagging and parsing);

definition an implementation of a reasoner to be applied on the annotations;

choice of a query language compatible with the reasoner, i.e. the query language should be powerful enough so that it can exploit the entire inference mechanism of the parser.

There are few projects in digital humanities which employ semantic representation of the data. One of the most prominent example is the CIDOC-CRM Ontology[2] a conceptual reference model for representing cultural heritage objects. Unfortunately the ontology is used mainly for encoding meta-data about the objects, but less for deep annotation of the content.

Another project using semantic relation between objects is Averroes[3], in which a corpus of all editions and translations of the philosopher Averroes are not only reproduced, but aligned by means of RDF-formalism.

The project „Inschriften im Bezugssystem des Raumes"[4] uses also RDF as formalism to represent different topologies of epigraphs and their interconnections.

We should mention also that currently, the PERSEUS[5] project containing the biggest collection of digitizes classical texts, is starting to release the data as LOD (Linked Open Data)[6] (Bridget et. al. 2014).

The projects mentioned above reached a certain degree of completion, and obviously there are some recent activities started. However, they represent a very small percent from the huge number of current digital humanities projects focused mainly on digitization and meta-data cataloguing.

Even the above mentioned projects do not consider a central aspect of humanities and in particular historical data: representation of vagueness. Meanwhile there are strong theoretical developments:

---

1 https://wordnet.princeton.edu/

2 http://www.cidoc-crm.org/official_release_cidoc.html

3 http://www.thomasinstitut.uni-koeln.de/11610.html?&L=0

4 http://www.digitale-akademie.de/projekte/inschriften-im-bezugssystem-des-raumes-ibr.html

5 http://www.perseus.tufts.edu/hopper/

6 http://linkeddata.org/

- inclusion of a module on certainty and precision in TEI;
- development of an ontology language including vagueness and
- corresponding implementations of reasoners and query languages.

However, to our knowledge, at least at the current moment they are not exploited by any project in digital humanities, although this is the only way to fully support humanists with new interpretations and analysis of their texts.

Manfred Thaller discusses already in (Thaller 1984) how relevant for historical research are the quantitative approaches, and insists for more computer-based formalisms which allows investigations lead by questions like "why fact X happened" (qualitative research) and not "how often fact X happened?" (quantitative research).

In (Thaller 2007) it is stated very clear that digitized texts as they are now realised are: not-ambiguous, context free and contain just the information embedded in the code, whilst historical texts are sequence of symbols, each carrying a meaning, which co-exist in a multidimensional space. These spaces are independent one of the other which makes possible to attach to each of them a metric.

These two works are seminal but with exception of them, digitization of data remains just a way of raw preservation: documents which can be read online. Search is related to words or in best case to words clusters, called wrongly concepts. This makes the computer just a static support for reading or in best case flat search, but does not imply it dynamical in the hermeneutic research. Progress in Computer science in the last years allows a change of paradigm.

2.3 Vagueness and Mark-up annotations

TEI[7] is currently the main standard used for encoding historical texts. The P5-Guidelines follow the XML-mark-up formalism and thus:

do not allow concurrent mark-up and

enable connections between annotated segments through Xlink-like pointers and unique identifiers.

TEI has a modular architecture: there is a core module with elements which can be used in all texts (most dealing with basic text structuring and formatting), as well as more than 20 modules covering almost all fields of textual humanities. The price paid for this broad coverage is an increased complexity in data representation, which triggers also difficulties in the parsing process.

Automatic Text processing tools cannot interpret TEI-Tags, thus these are filtered out, together with useful information contained by their semantics (Piotrowski 2012, pag.66).

TEI offers three possibilities for encoding vagueness:

1. the <note> element: the user can write unstructured text, mentioning the degree and scope of the vague aspect identified);
2. the <certainty> element: this offers the possibility to structure the information about vagueness. The <certainty> element can refer to the name of the annotation tag considered uncertain (e.g. a person or a place name), the position in text where the annotation tag starts, or a value of an attribute contained in the annotation tag). Through the attribute @degree it is possible to refine the level of certainty. The <certainty> element can refer to one or more annotation elements through XPath expressions;
3. The <precision> element, which can be applied for any numerical value (a date, or a measure). It indicates the numerical accuracy associated to some aspects of a text mark-up. If a standard value is precise and known, one can express it with the element <precision> and the attribute @stdDev, which represents its standard deviation.

Additional TEI offers the possibility to indicate the responsible for the whole content or partial annotators. In this way one can specify if the vagueness is due to the author, the quoted source or the editor.

TEI-P5 specifications mention that. "The certainty element allows for indications to be structures with at least as much detail and clarity as appears to be currently required in most ongoing text projects" As mentioned before, TEI is mainly used for encoding text as near as possible to the original and display it. Rarely deep queries are performed on the annotation, also because it is practically impossible to have a general parser, which allows

7 http://www.tei-c.org/Guidelines/P5/

complex queries. TEI parsers are usually dedicated, e.g. deal with the core module and a certain domain.

There are several drawbacks of the TEI approach for annotating vagueness:

1. Overlapping annotations concerning vagueness are possible only as stand-off annotation. However stand-off annotation in TEI is extremely complicated.

2. There are different levels of vagueness introduced by the author by the referred source, dating etc. Not all these sources of vagueness can be specified with the <respons> tag which can be attached just to individuals.

3. <precision> can be specified just for numerical values. An expression "some kilometres south from the city" introduce a non-numerical vague coordinate. When we speak about historical documents, sometimes even geo-location of the place is not possible.

4. There is no reasoner which can be applied to the TEI annotation.

2.4 *2.4. Vagueness in Ontological modelling*

A semantic model for historical data should imply a mapping to at least a domain ontology. OWL[8] (Web Ontology language) is the current standard used for expressing ontological knowledge. One can specify classes, subclasses, properties and subproperties, roles and can relate all these together through logical statements from Description Logic. OWL assertions are specified following the RDF-triple formalism (Subject-Predicate-Object). The OWL was used intensively in the first generation applications of Semantic Web. However, it became obvious that it is a common requirement in real world applications that the system is able to deal with imprecise /vague knowledge, which cannot be modelled with OWL (Bobillo et al 2012).

In order to simulate vague knowledge, methods as Reification[9] or Named Graphs[10] were used. However they have two drawbacks:

- Increase (sometimes dramatically) the number of RDF-triple

- At the end, they rely again on crisp description logic.

The new OWL 2 standard offers the possibility of designing fuzzy Ontologies and realize inferences with fuzzy logic. The principle is to use an OWL 2 ontology, extending its elements with annotation properties representing the features of the fuzzy ontology that OWL 2 cannot directly encode (Bobillo and Straccia 2010). With this formalism one can define vague expressions as fuzzy modifiers and apply them to data-types and concepts. In OWL 2 Concepts can receive also weights.

For example to define the concept (0.8 A + 0.2 B): one creates the atomic "Sum08Aplus02B" and annotate it:

```
  Class ( Sum08Aplus02B Annotation
          ( fuzzyLabel
                    <              fuzzyOwl2
fuzzyType =" concept " >
                    < Concept type ="
weightedSum " >
                    < Concept type ="
weighted " value ="0.8" base =" A " /
>
                     < Concept type ="
weighted " value ="0.2" base =" B " /
>
     ))
```

For the creation of a fuzzy ontology a Protégé[11] API the Fuzzy Ontology Editor[12] is freely available. The plug-in is generic and not specific to any reasoner. In the next section, we show how this can be pipelined with a reasoner.

2.5 Vagueness and reasoning

Most used reasoner for fuzzy ontologies is the DELOREAN reasoner (Bobillo et al. 2013). The reasoning algorithms within this system, are based on the computation of a crisp ontology that preserves the semantics of the original fuzzy ontology and therefore reasoning with the former is equivalent with the latter. The developers of the DELOREAN reasoner applied successfully the same principle for Zadeh as well as Gödel fuzzy description logic.

8 https://www.w3.org/2001/sw/wiki/OWL

9 https://www.w3.org/DesignIssues/Reify.html

10 https://www.w3.org/2004/03/trix/

11 http://protege.stanford.edu/

12 http://www.umbertostraccia.it/cs/software/FuzzyOWL/

The equivalent crisp ontology is larger than the fuzzy one, as additional axioms have to be added in order to keep the semantics.

The DELOREAN reasoner can be used as a standard application or through the provided API integrated in a larger system.

An important contribution to mathematical modelling of vague data is given in (Schlarb 2008). The definition of certain operators still has to be compared with the formalism offered by fuzzy OWL.

2.6 Automatic processing of historical texts

Language technology (LT) reached a certain maturity during last years. Industrial applications use now LT component for modern languages, like lemmatisers, PoS Tagging, Named entity Recognizers (Vertan and v Hahn 2012). The picture is different when referring to historical languages. Moreover, for one modern language, there are several historical variants and the borders between them are not really clear. Additionally, languages became standardized in the late XVIIth-XIXth century, so there are not clear rules to be encoded. A big problem is also the orthography which was not completely standardized, so many variants may occur for the same word. Without any pre-processing step, no modern language processing tool can be applied to historical variants.

Minimal transformations imply orthographic normalization and in some cases syntactic translation rules (Piotrowski 2012). Less attention is paid to semantics and the conceptual space (thus implicit knowledge) which changed during the years (Vertan 2010) (Vertan and v. Hahn 2014a).

Many historical documents present a document multilinguality: there are words or paragraphs at least in Latin or classical Greek. These paragraphs have to be identified and isolated prior to any other processing.

.

3 Rationale of the corpus

Dimitrie Cantemir (1673-1623) was prince of Moldavia (historical region including regions from current eastern part of Romania, Republic of Moldavia and some parts from Ukraine), man of letters-philosopher, historian, musicologist, linguist, ethnographer and geographer. He received education in classical studies (Greek and Latin in his country of origin), then he lived for several years in Istanbul where he learned Turkish, and familiarized himself with the cultural traditions of the ottomans, meet important persons around the sultan and learned a lot about history of the Empire. After a very short period of being prince of Moldavia he was forced to immigrate to Russia, where he became an important person at the court of Tsar Peter the Great. During this period, his works gained attention in the Western countries. He became member of the Royal Academy in Berlin and, at their request, he produced the two books which are the subject of this proposal:

Descriptio antiqui et hodierni status Moldaviae, written in Latin, a history of his country in which he describes not only pure historical facts but also traditions, the language, the political and administration system. Local denominations and troponins, as well as names are written in Romanian with Latin script as his intention is to demonstrate the Latin origin of his folk. The transcriptions are not standardized and one retrieves for the same troponin several name variations. Quotations as known today are very rare, there is no bibliography. According to (Lemny 2010), as there was practically no consistent previous work about the region, Cantemir himself was not particularly careful with indicating sources of knowledge. The work is accompanied by a map, the first detailed cartography of the region. The names on the map are in Romanian language. The Latin original was translated for the first time in German, and only later at the middle of the XIXth century in Romanian. The Latin manuscript seemed to be lost for a long time, so that the first Romanian translation was following the German one. The German translation is containing editorial notes of the translator.

Historia incrementorum atque decrementorum Aulae Othomanicae, the history of the Ottoman Empire. In contrast with the previous work about Moldavia, here Cantemir indicates very carefully the sources of information. (Lemny 2010) supposes the existence of previous works, known in the western countries, behind this decision. This work was written also at the request of the Academy in Berlin. Cantemir follows the same principle: text in Latin, while the troponins and local denominations are written this time in Ottoman Turkish. Although there were already some previous works about the Ottoman Empire, the novelty of his approach is the quotation of Turkish sources. The reliability of these sources is untrusted sometimes by Cantemir himself. The manuscript reaches the western world after Cantemir's death, carried by his son to London. Here, a first translation in English is produced: The history of Raise and Decay of the Ottoman Empire. The translator reinterprets the texts, probably also being confused by the presence of Turkish information sources, which were perceived in that time as completely unreliable. The Latin original remains lost for centuries and is rediscovered only at the end of the XXth century in the USA. Thus, the German translation is based on the English one and inherits the same alterations, and presumably adds new ones. The Romanian translations use in contrast the Latin original. The last translation (Costa 2015a) will be used in this proposal.

Until now there is no systematic study on the reliability of the text sources in Cantemir's works, nor the degree of alterations produced by the translations of the two works.

Given the fact that both works became standard reference for western authors until the middle of XIXth century, it is expected that their reception influenced also following historical material. There is no reprint / new edition of his works in German or English. There are however, several reprints of the Romanian versions. Recent Romanian translations of Decriptio Moldaviae are done after the original Latin manuscript.

A lot of works were dedicated to the personality of Dimitrie Cantemir and its perception in different parts of Europe. A study of the reliability and consistency of the historical facts as they are described in originals and their translations is practically impossible to be done only with traditional hermeneutic methods. One needs expertise in the same time in Latin, German, English, Romanian, Turkish, just to enumerate the main languages used in the two books, which additionally sum up to a volume of about 1000 pages. Both German editions are printed in "Fraktur" script, which is nowadays very difficult to be read. A recent digitalization done by the BBAW for the History of the Ottoman Empire13, makes the text more accessible. The digital version is freely available in TEi-P5 format. However, the TEI-P5 concentrates only on a diplomatic transcription and a flat linguistic annotation (lemma and part of speech) and does not touch any aspects of vagueness or reliability of sources.

Cantemir's texts are a real challenge with respect to multilinguality: in Descriptio Moldaviae,

[13]http://www.deutschestextarchiv.de/book/show/cantemir_geschichte_1745

4 Workflow for annotation of vagueness

For the particular corpus presented in section 3 we decided to represent vagueness and other types of uncertainty at least five levels

1. the text uncertainty (uncertain readings, losses, translations, multilinguality, etc.),
2. the linguistic vagueness (metonymies, vague adjectives, comparatives, non-intersectives, hedges, homonyms,),
3. the author reliability (genres, time style, general recognition),
4. the factual uncertainty (range expressions, time expressions, geo relations), and
5. historical change (named entities, abbreviations, meaning changes).

In a first phase we collect for each of the processed languages (German, Romanian and Latin) explicit lexical vagueness markers like words or expressions such as:

- Vague quanitfiers, e.g.: some, most of, a few, about, etc.
- Modal adverbs, e.g.: probably, possibly, etc.
- Verbs e.g.: to believe, think, prefer, etc.
- Lexical quotation markers , e.g. introduced by quotation marks or verbs with explicit meaning (say, write, mention)
- Inexact measures and cardinals
- Complex quantifiers
- Non-intersective adjectives
- Implicit syntactic clues: mainly verb moods such as conditional-optative for Romanian, conjunctive mood or imperfect/pluperfect for Latin, all of them indicating a non-reality (doubt, hear-say, possibility, etc.)

To annotate vague expressions like the ones above, the first step is to (semi-automatically) identify them. Identifying the three distinct categories of expressions that induce vagueness (explicit-lexical, implicit-syntactic and pragmatic) requires different strategies.

To automatically identify (mark up in text) the explicit lexical-semantic clues, our strategy is the following: one manually create a list of words and expressions that are possible indicators of vagueness for the three languages (Latin, Romanian and German), from selected parts of texts. After the preprocessing step (chunking, lemmatizing, PoS tagging, NP-chunking), based on the previously created list, one automatically finds and marks all the (inflected forms of) explicit vagueness terms. Finally, one manually checks the marking for a short part of text for evaluation, followed by feedback and slight improvement.

The automatic identification of syntactic clues is a much more difficult/complex task. There is an inherent ambiguity in the text between vagueness and plain quotation (often intentionally created by the author) that is difficult to decide upon even for a human annotator, and thus impossible for the machine. A possible strategy to be investigated is: to use machine learning techniques (may be the power of deep learning) on a training set of positive examples obtained from explicit clues and negative examples of certain text.

A clear indicator of vagueness are also named entities like persons and places, especially when they differ in transliteration, spelling within the text or across similar historical sources. Thus the annotation of named entitiees is of central role.

However the unclear person, time, place identification is even more difficult to automatize or at least assist by computer techniques, being more of a matter of hermeneutical research for humanists and historians.

5 Conclusions and further work

Annotation and interpretation of vagueness is a central issue in digital processing of historical texts. However this issue was completely neglected until now, and has as consequence often distorted interpretation of digitized historical texts. In this article we presented the current state of the art on vagueness annotation and introduce the first approached for considering vague expressions as part of the annotation process. Further work concerns the automatic annotation of such expressions, the construction of the ontology and the implementation of the interpretation layer.

Acknowledgements

Research described in this article is supported by HerCoRe project, funded by Volkswagen Foundation (Project no. 91970)

Bibliography

Fernando Bobillo, and Umberto Straccia, 2010, *"Fuzzy Ontology Representation using OWL 2"*, http://arxiv.org/pdf/1009.3391.pdf (last retrieved 15.02.2016)

Fernando Bobillo, and Miguel Delgado, and Juan Gomez-Romero, 2013, *"Reasoning in Fuzzy OWL 2 with DeLorean, in Uncertainity,* Reasoning for the Semantic Web II, Bobillo, F.,Costa, P.C.G.,d'Amato, C.,Fanizzi, N.,Laskey, K.B.,Laskey, K.J.,Lukasiewicz, Th.,Nickles, M.,Pool, M. (Eds.), Lecture Notes in Artificial Intelligence, Springer Verlag

Almas Bridget and Alison Babeu, Alison and Anna Krohn, 2014, *„Linked data in the erseus Digital Library"*, ISAW Papers 7.3, http://dlib.nyu.edu/awdl/isaw/isaw-papers/7/almas-babeu-krohn/ (last retrieved 15.02.2016)

Dimitrie Cantemir 1771, Beschreibung der Moldau, Faksimiledruck der Originalausgabe von 1771, Frankfurt und Leipzig

Dimitrie Cantemir 1745, Dimitrie, Geschichte des osmanischen Reichs nach seinem Anwachse und Abnehmen, 1745, Herold, Hamburg

Ioana Costa 2015, Dimitrie Cantemir, Istoria măririi şi decăderii Curţii othmane, 2 volume, editarea textului latinesc şi aparatul critic Octavian Gordon, Florentina Nicolae, Monica Vasileanu, traducere din limba latină Ioana Costa, cuvânt înainte Eugen Simion, studiu introductiv Ştefan Lemny, Bucureşti, Academia Română-Fundaţia Naţională pentru Ştiinţă şi Artă, 2015. ISBN 978-606-555-135-0 (978-606-555-136-7, 978-606-555-137-4)

Stefan Lemny, 2010, Cantemirestii -Aventura europeana a unei familii princiare din secolul al XVIII-lea, Polirom Publishing House.

Florentina Nicolae 2004, Toponime si Hidronime in literature Cantemiriana, Annals of Philology XV, pag., 143-152

Manfred Pinkal, 1980, *Semantische Vagheit: Phänomene und Theorien*. In: Linguistische Berichte 70. 1980. 1-26. und 72. 1981. 1-26.

Manfred Pinkal 1985, *Logik und Lexikon*: Die Semantik des Unbestimmten.

Michael Piotrowski 2012, „Natural Language Processing for Historical Texts", Morgan & Claypool Publishers, Synthesis Lectures on human Language Technologies.

Sven Schlarb, 2008 *Unscharfe Validierung strukturierten Daten –ein Model auf basis unscharfer Logik*, Köllner Beiträge zu einer geisteswissenschaftlichen Fachinformatik, Band 1,

Manfred Thaller 1984, *„Ungefähre Exaktheit. Theoretische Grundlagen und Praktische Möglichkeiten einer Formulierung historischer Quellen als Produkte ‚unscharfer' Systeme"*, in Neue Ansätze in der Geschichtswissenschaft, Conceptus Studien 1, Wien, pp. 77-100

Manfred Thaller 2007 *„Was macht einen Quellentext für die Informatik ‚historisch'?"*, in De litteris, manuscriptis, inscriptionibus ... Festschrift zum 65. Geburtstag von Walter Koch, Kölzer, Theo and Friedl, Christian and Vogeler, Georg (Eds.), Wien-Köln-Weimar 2007, pp. 543-557

Cristina Vertan and Walther v. Hahn 2012, "*Multilingual Processing in Eastern and Southern EU Languages: Low-Resourced Technologies and Translation*". 396 pages. Cambridge Scholars Publishers. Newcastle

Cristina Vertan and Walther v. Hahn 2014, *Discovering and Explaining Knowledge in Historical Documents*, In: Kristin Bjnadottir, Stewen Krauwer, Cristina Vertan and Martin Wyne (Eds.), Proceedings of the Workshop on "Language Technology for Historical Languages and Newspaper Archives"associated with LREC 2014, Reykjavik Mai 2014, p. 76-80.

Cristina Vertan and Walther v. Hahn 2014, *Making historical texts accessible to everybody*. Dublin Workshop für Text Simplification. Dublin 2014

Cristina Vertan and Walther v. Hahn 2014, *Das Balkanbild in Deutschland während der letzten 300 Jahre - Eine digitale Plattform zu Analyse und Erschließung multilingualer Dokumente über die Balkanländer und das Osmanische Reich*, In: Proceedings of the Digital Humanities- Germany Conference, 25-28 March 2014, Passau, Germany

Cristina Vertan 2010, *Towards the Integration of Language Tools Within Historical Digital Libraries"*, in Proceedings of the international Conference for Language Ressources and Evaluation LREC 2010, Malta, 19-21May 2010

Cristina Vertan and Walther v. Hahn 2015, *Multilinguality in Historical Texts - Applying Language Technology for Cultural Heritage* , Charles university of Prague. (http://ufal.mff.cuni.cz/events/seminar-35th-anniversary-cooperation-between-charles-university-prague-and-hamburg-university)

Walther v. Hahn 2015 *Preserving Vagueness: The Central Mission of Next Generation Digital Humanities*. Charles university of Prague. (http://ufal.mff.cuni.cz/events/seminar-35th-anniversary-cooperation-between-charles-university-prague-and-hamburg-university

Language Technologies in Teaching Bulgarian at Primary and Secondary School Level: The NBU Platform for Language Teaching (PLT)

Maria Stambolieva, Milka Hadjikoteva, Mariya Neykova
(Laboratory for Language Technologies, NBU),
Valentina Ivanova, Mariana Raykova (Digital Innovation Laboratory, NBU)

Abstract

The NBU Language Teaching Platform (PLT) is a versatile tool supporting language learning. So far used for FLSP e-tuition or blended learning in general foreign language classes, it is now being extended to provide e-support for teaching Bulgarian at primary and secondary school level. Methodologically, it compensates for some of the major drawbacks of the functional/CLT approaches to language teaching. The article presents the general structure of the platform and the functionalities specifically developed to match the standards and expected results set by the Bulgarian Ministry of Education.

1 Aim of the project

The Platform for Language Teaching (PLT) was developed as a teaching tool enhancing the Moodle-supported e-tuition for blended learning at NBU, as a complement to the standard communicative methods of the language classroom. It was designed by a team of university experts in the field of pedagogy and the methodology of foreign language learning and was initially devised as a necessary supplement to foreign language classes. In view of its new application to Bulgarian language teaching at primary and secondary school level, new corpora and functionalities are now being developed in accordance with standards and programs recently published by the Bulgarian Ministry of Education[1], and with the new challenges posed by the need to teach Bulgarian (language skills, basic linguistic knowledge and familiarity with Bulgarian literature) to students for whom it is not a native language. The platform provides individualised tuition for students who prefer to work on their own, at their own pace. Monitoring is fast and precise, giving teachers and students detailed feedback on overall performance and specific errors.

2 Methodological issues

The PLT offers teaching material and drills which complement the functional/CLT method of first/second language classes by compensating for some often noted drawbacks[2], namely:

- insufficient attention to structure and form;
- preference for fluency over accuracy;
- unsystematic presentation and drilling of grammar;
- insufficient drilling of vocabulary;
- reliance on group and pair work (which is not appropriate to all classroom environments and students);

---

[1] http://zareformata.mon.bg/documents/naredba_6_11.08.2016_bg_ezik.pdf, www.mon.bg/?h=downloadFile&fileId=546

[2] Cf. Langeveldt, H., 2012. Communicative Language Teaching (CLT): Strengths and Weaknesses. Accessed at: https://issuu.com/miriamsheen/docs/_clt_strengths_and_weaknesses; Sumhachalam Thamarana 2015. A Critical Overview of Communicative Language Teaching. International Journal of English Language Literature and Humanities, vol. III, Issue V, July 2015. Accessed at https://www.researchgate.net/publication/282877159_A_Critical_Overview_of_Communicative_Language_Teaching.

Proceedings of the LT4DHCSEE in conjunction with RANLP 2017, pages 32–38,
Varna, Bulgaria, 8 September 2017.

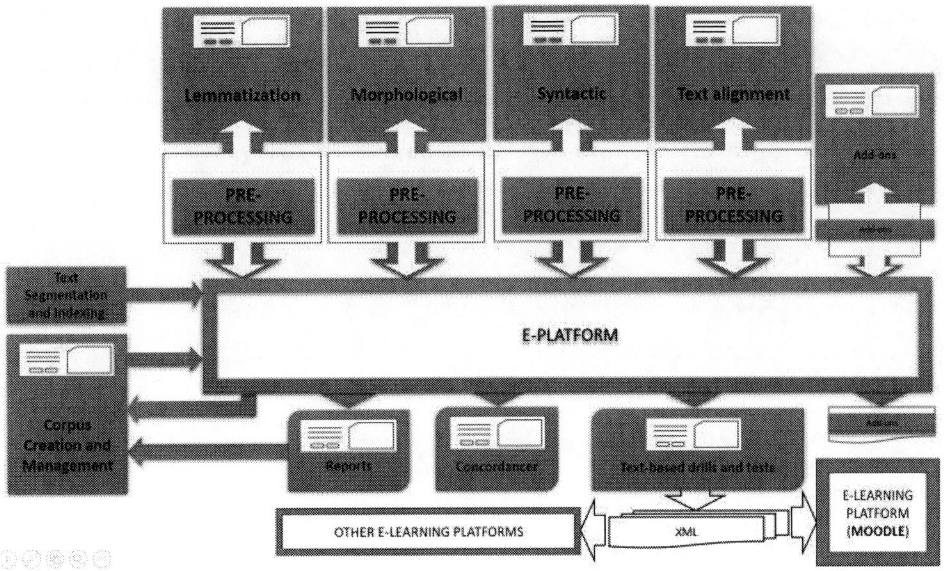

Figure 1. Structure of the platform: modules

- toleration of errors (seen by CLT as a natural part of the process of language learning);
- exclusion of the student's native language;
- inappropriateness for beginners;
- problems of monitoring.

The new functions of the PLT as a tool for Bulgarian language teaching as both a native and second/foreign language require the development of a new corpus and a new data base, the design of new sets of drills on:

- Bulgarian vocabulary (general vocabulary and terms[3], multi-word lexemes, collocations and phraseological units);
- Bulgarian practical grammar (gender, number, plurality of nouns and noun satellites, use of prepositions, verbal Aktionsart, aspect, tense, word order, etc.);
- Basic linguistic knowledge (of morphology and syntax — for students in the 6th and 7th class);
- Familiarity with literary texts.

The tests are based on excerpts from the literary works recommended for the respective class/educational level; the choice of texts and exercise types for the two educational levels and groups of target students are consulted with experts from the regional inspectorates of education.

3 Structure of the platform

In accordance with its aims and functions, the PLT integrates: 1/ an environment for creating, organising and maintaining electronic text; for extracting text corpora and aligning corpora; 2/ a linguistic database; 3/ a set of modules for the generation and editing of practice exercises for each text or corpus; 4/ functionalities for export from the platform and import to other educational platforms (Figure 1). Special modules have been created for test generation, performance assessment and feedback, allowing thus not only centralised presentation of abundant teaching content, but also control of the educational process, plus fast and reliable feedback on performance[4].

`The PLT is a web-based system developed using a model-view-controller (MVC) open source framework – CodeIgniter and PHP programming language. The framework provides the core implementation of the interdependences and the interdependences and the interactions between the three tiers of the MVC architecture, while the de-

[3] The Ministry of Education does not offer clear standards for vocabulary skills. For each grade and class, we base our general vocabulary and terminology drills on textbooks and recommended literature.

[4] Cf. also M. Stambolieva, M. Hadjikoteva, M. Neykova, M. Raykova, V. Ivanova 2017.

Figure 2. Platform navigation menu – access to the modules.

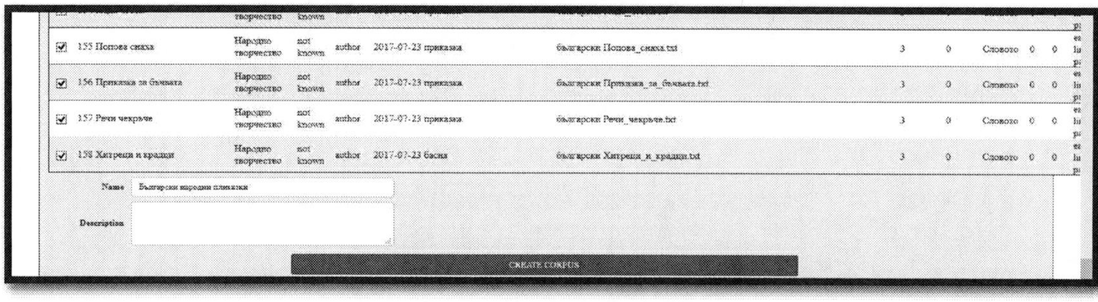

Figure 3. Grouping texts into corpora

velopers focus on the PLT specific features.

The MVC modular architecture is selected for its extensibility, supportability, scalability, and maintainability. The modules of the platform are implemented following the convention:

- controllers: class ModuleName, extends CI_Controller, file name ModuleName.php;
- models: class ModuleName_model, extends CI_Model, file name ModuleName_model.php;
- views: folder ModuleName, a corresponding .php file for each item from the items list of the module: index.php, create.php, etc.

The PLT stores the linguistic data in a relational database with 46 tables implemented on MySQL.

To provide enhanced user experience and ease of use, the PLT user-interface design is uniform for all modules. PLT look-and-feel is implemented using CSS3. The interaction between the system and the users is direct synchronous on load of the module and asynchronous communication through AJAX requests for in-module data management and updates.

The PLT is designed for extensibility and scalability. The platform may easily integrate:

- new modules for collecting linguistic data;
- new modules for generating new types of exercises;
- export to new e-learning platforms in addition to the export to MOODLE.

Finally, the PLT could be utilized as a research platform.

4 PLT modules and features

4.1 Creating texts and corpora

The environment for the maintenance of the electronic text archive organises a variety of metadata: bibliographical information on the publication, professional area of the publication, text difficulty – with recommended level of the European language framework. These metadata, either individually or in different combinations, form the basis for the extraction of text corpora. Linguistic analysis is performed on either a single text or a corpus of texts; at any time, corpora can be expanded with additional texts from the archive or in other ways reorganized, without loss of linguistic information.

The word form lists generated by the platform and the results of lemmatisation are used to derive vocabulary lists for the respective educational level. General vocabulary words or terms can be provided with definitions, synonyms or translations, to be used for the generation of multiple matching exercises[5].

[5] For the methodological foundations of the project and the design of the exercises, Cf. M.S. Hadjikoteva 2005 and M. Neykova 2014.

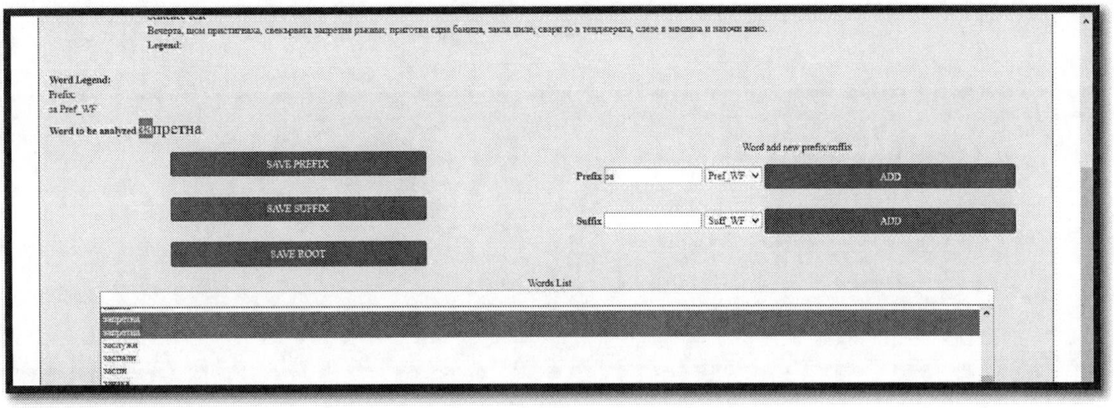

Figure 4. Morphemic analysis

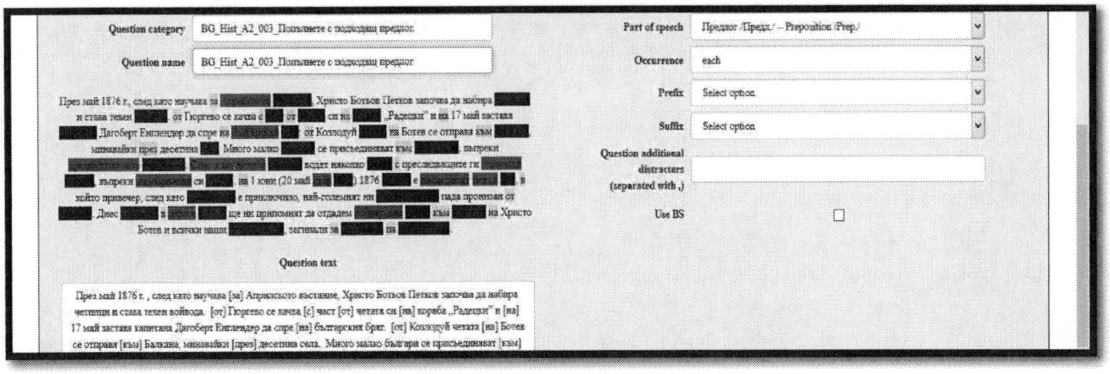

Figure 5. Generating a Multiple choice exercise
(Fill in the blanks with an appropriate Preposition).

4.2 The linguistic database

The PLT includes an up-to-date system of modules designed in the spirit of an earlier Linguist's Workbench package[6], but integrated here into a new linguistic data base[7]. The corpora are lemmatised and POS-tagged, morphemically and syntactically analysed. Selected vocabulary items are provided with simple definitions, synonyms or translations (Figure 4).

4.3 Generating practice exercises

The linguistic data base allows the generation of a large number of language drills. Most of these appear in the format of standard Open the brackets, Open cloze, Multiple choice, Multiple matching or Reorder the words/sentences/paragraphs exercises (Figure 5). Newly developed options are based on the results of the morphemic and syntactic analyzers (Open cloze or multiple choice exercises with derivational or inflexional affixes or roots; multiple matching exercises for word form - part of speech pairs; word form-grammatical category pairs; phrase-syntactic function pairs).

Drills are based on one or more paragraphs from the corpus. The paragraphs need not be consecutive and can even come from different texts.

The generation of an exercise is based on the choice of a specific set of options. For the multiple choice exercise above, the set of options chosen is POS: Preposition, Occurrence: each, Lemma: unticked (i.e. the lemma will not appear). A further choice relates to the format: Gapfill, Drag-and-drop or DropdownFormat.

The platform also allows the generation of vocabulary drills of the multiple matching type, based on definition, synonymy or, also, translation (for non-native speakers of the language).

For reordering exercises, the following options are available: word in sentence (suitable for both primary and secondary school level), sentences in paragraph and paragraphs in text, syntactic phrases in sentence/clause (suitable for secondary school level) (Figure 6).

[6] M. Stambolieva 1996, M. Stambolieva, and D. Dragostinov 2014.
[7] M. Raykova, V. Ivanova 2017

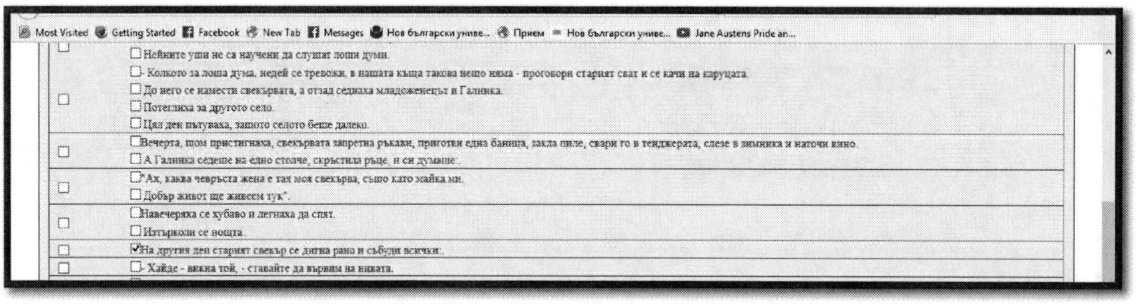

Figure 6. Generating a Reordering exercise (sentences in paragraph).

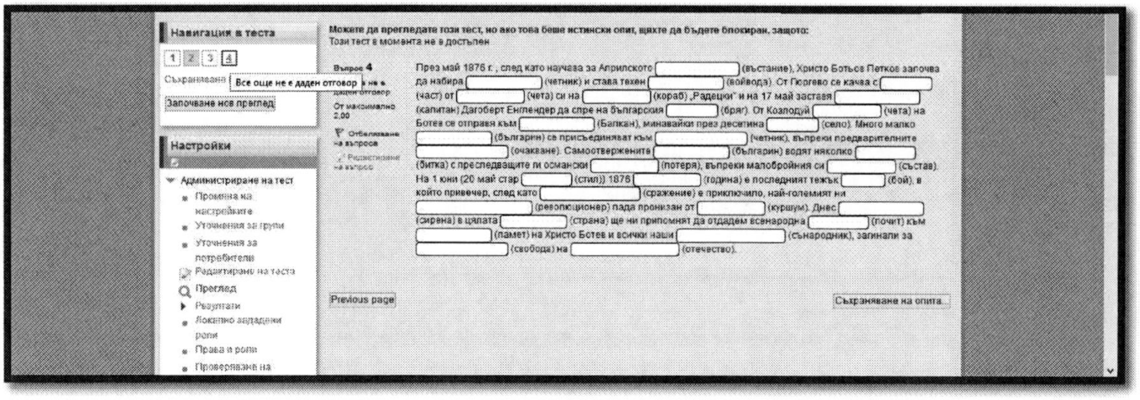

Figure 7. An Open-the-brackets exercises (ticked Lemma)

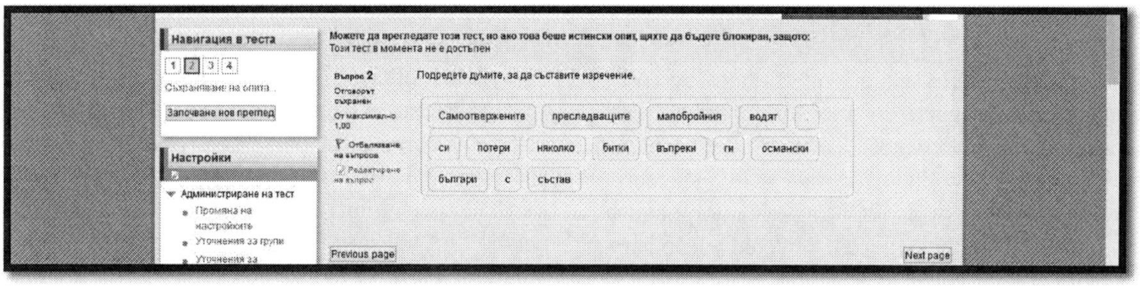

Figure 8. A reordering exercise (words in sentence).

5 From the PLT to other educational platforms

The training exercises generated in the E-platform can be exported to other educational platforms. There, the exercises can be organised in archives attached to each level (language level or class) and can be combined to form tests. Figures 7 and 8 illustrate the visualisation of the exercises in Moodle.

5.1 Student performance assessment

The results of students' performance are generated automatically, with quantitative information for each student and group statistics. Students, teachers, headmasters or higher institutions (regional inspectorates, Ministry of Education administrators and others) can receive immediate feedback for each student/class/school, for each separate task and for the test overall. This feedback offers a mechanism of control and can be used in identifying areas of difficulty, underperforming students, classes and schools (Figure 9 and 10).

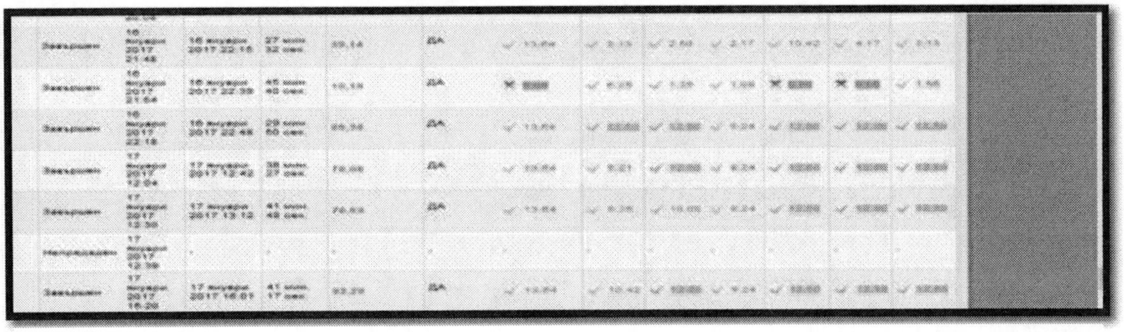

Figure 9. Feedback on performance

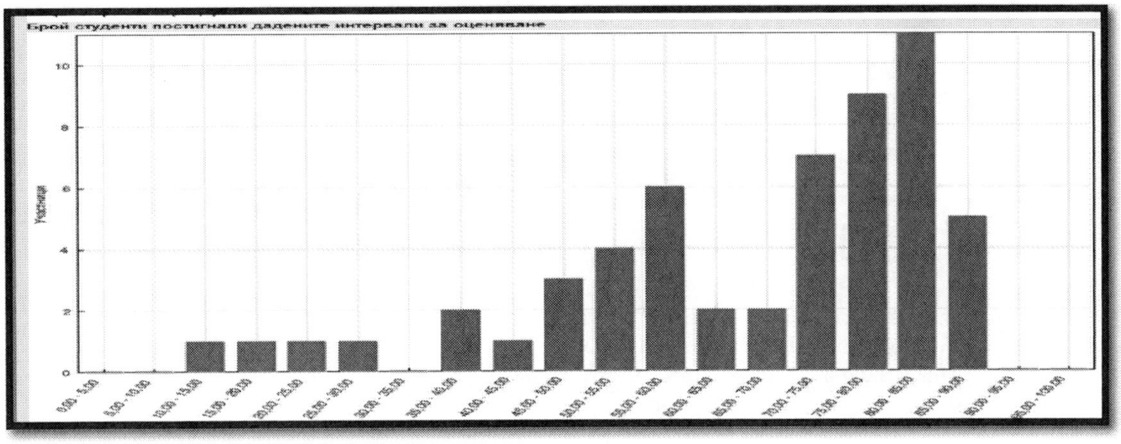

Figure 10. Statistical information on student performance

6 Conclusions and future work

The PLT offers a variety of options for corpus creation and corpus-based or text-based generation of educational content for one or more languages. It combines the general advantages of e-learning with blended learning and teaching supplementation to function-oriented or communicative teaching in the language classroom.

The flexible design of the system and its multiple functionalities make it an appropriate tool for e-teaching of native or second/foreign languages at all educational levels.

The corpus and educational content presented are designed for the specific needs of teaching Bulgarian and will be tested in the course of the school year 2017/2008.

References

Hadjikoteva, M. S. 2005. Types of Students and Relevant Input. *BETA-IATEFL Conference Proceedings.* (2005). Retrieved May 2017 from http://www.beta-iatefl.org/1109/blog-publications/types-of-students-and-relevant-input/

Langeveldt, H. 2012. Communicative Language Teaching (CLT): Strengths and Weaknesses. Retrieved May 2017 from: : https://issuu.com/miriamsheen/docs/_clt_strengths_and_weaknesses

Neykova, M. 2014. An Action-oriented Approach in the Context of Blended Learning. *BETA E-Newsletter*. Retrieved 2017 from http://www.beta-iatefl.org/cogitoergosum/wp-content/uploads/2014/12/BETA_E-Newsletter_November_December_2014.pdf

Raykova, M., Ivanova, V. 2017. *NBU E-Platform in Teaching Foreign Languages for Specific Purposes – Software Engineering Challenges*. Proceedings of the 13th Annual International Conference on Computer Science and Education in Computer Science. Petya Assenova, Vijaj Kanabar (eds.) New Bulgarian University, Hochschule Fulda University of Applied Science, Boston University.

Sumhachalam T. 2015. A Critical Overview of Communicative Language Teaching. *International Journal of English Language Literature and Humanities*, vol. III, Issue V, July 2015. Accessed at https://www.researchgate.net/publication/282877159_A_Critical_Overview_of_Communicative_Language_Teaching.

Stambolieva M. A 1996. *Linguist's Workbench*. Papers from the First Conference on Formal Approaches to South Slavic Languages. University of Trondheim Working Papers in Linguistics 28, p. 293 – 301.

Stambolieva, M., Dragostinov, D. 2014. *The NBU Linguist's Workbench*. Proceedings of the 10th Annual International Conference on Computer Science and Education in Computer Science. Petya Assenova, Vijaj Kanabar (eds.) New Bulgarian University, Hochschule Fulda University of Applied Science, Boston University, p. 259-266.

Stambolieva, M., Hadjikoteva, M., Neykova, M., Raykova, M., Ivanova V. 2017. *The NBU E-Platform in Teaching Foreign Languages for Specific Purposes*. Proceedings of the 13th Annual International Conference on Computer Science and Education in Computer Science. Petya Assenova, Vijaj Kanabar (eds.) New Bulgarian University, Hochschule Fulda University of Applied Science, Boston University

Personalization of Political Discoures On Social Media

Cristina Florentina Moise, University of Bucharest, cristi-
na.florentina.moise@gmail.com

Abstract

According to Phillips and Young, success in politics is now highly influenced by the online activities of political institutions. Within these platforms, politicians can exchange views on the latest partisan developments or hot topics, inviting the public and citizens to comment, share ideas and adhere to their political programs [Phililips and Young et al 2009].

According to Sundar, Kalyanaraman, and Brown (2003) interactivity is usually associated with positive perception. The user will only make an effort to search and read the information if he feels engaged with the political party or message [Sundar, Kalyanaraman and Brown et al 2003]. Online political engagement is largely restricted to people already active in politics and on the Internet. Other audiences are less responsive [Tenhunen and Karvelyte et al 2015].

Nevertheless, in the last years, social media has reshaped its structures and methods of contemporary political communication. The public became more active and willing to react to political message even though it is not partisan of a political party.

That is why, in the last years, politicians have a significant interest to have a two-way communication with their citizens, to discover their opinions and feelings about different ideas. Therefore, it is essential to allocate resources for sentiment analysis, which is also called opinion mining (one of the most active research areas in natural language processing since early 2000 [Liu et al 2012]).

1 Introduction

Online environment especially, social media channels are the most used tools for public communication within societies. In particular, for having a direct dialog with their citizens, politicians are continuously delivering message on microblogs (like Twitter) or on social networks (like Facebook) [Chilton and Schäffner et al 2002].

For political communication, it is essential to come with personalized discourses for each segment of voters, to get the insights quickly and to have the flexibility to adapt the message according to the context and to the people reaction.

This paper overviews the Majoritas ecosystem (https://majoritas.com/), providing a complete overview of political campaigns assessment aimed to assist politicians and their staff in delivering consistent and personalized message.

The system has been running for five years being adopted on almost all continents: Brazil, the US, France, Congo, Indonesia, Moldavia, Albania, Serbia, etc.

The ecosystem contains a suite of services and applications that can outline and summarize data provided by online, offline and social media sources, assists in creating the right message to the right audience, assessing voters' behavior during the entire time of the campaign.

The solution was built to help politicians to have an iterative approach in their campaigns. It is important to adopt an 'agile' methodology when political communication strategy is defined. After each message, post or tweet, politicians need to assess the impact. What is the reaction of their followers or, is there any response from the competition?

Majoritas Social Media Room (one of the application of Majoritas ecosystem) was designed as a cloud political communication platform that assists politicians in empowering their social media presence. In other words, from a single place, the candidate can communicate diverse types of mes-

Proceedings of the LT4DHCSEE in conjunction with RANLP 2017, pages 39–43,
Varna, Bulgaria, 8 September 2017.

sage within his social media community using multiple Twitter accounts and Facebook pages.

Besides delivering messages, Social Media platform was designed to get real time voters' reaction regarding candidate's posts and tweets, providing insights concerning their engagement to different topics, ideas or beliefs.

2 Related Work

Mullen and Malouf et al 2006, based on the posts collected from several political blogs, tried to classify if posters' orientation was either left or right. They applied the Naïve Bayes text classifier and conclude that for political sentiment analysis, the traditional word-based text classification is not adequate.

According to Yu and Hatzivassiloglou et al 2003, considering the character limitation of tweets, classifying the sentiment analysis of Twitter messages is similar to the analysis of sentence-level sentiment. It is important to consider the informal tone as well and the specialized language used on social media.

Besides sentiment analysis algorithms, TF-IDF (Term Frequency-Inverse Document Frequency) technique is also very useful to performing microblogs text mining.

Even though both: sentiment analysis and TF-IDF are considered text classification techniques, their scope is different. On the one hand, the aim of sentiment analysis is to classify texts into opinions: 'negative' or 'positive'. On the other hand, the scope of TF-IDF is to classify categories within categories.

TF-IDF calculates a weight which represents the importance of a term inside a text:
TF(t) = (Number of times term t appears in a document) / (Total number of terms in the document)
IDF(t) = log_e(Total number of documents / Number of documents with term t in it).

Value = TF * IDF

Another important aspect that needs to be considered in translating microblogs messages into insights regarding posters' feelings, views, judgements, is the social network. As per Pozzi, Fersini, Mesina and Liu et al 2017, sentiment analysis in social networks is generally based on the assumption that the texts provided by the users are independent and identically distributed.

The principle of homophily [Lazarsfeld and Merton et al 1954], reveals that based on the 'friendship' relationships, connected users may be likelier to share similar opinions.

Popescu and Etzioni et al 2005 proposed PMI - Pointwise Mutual Information statistics to improve aspect extraction on product reviews. They introduced the meronymy term which represents a part-whole relationship. In regard to politics, the topics used by candidates in their discourse are also a form of meronymy since these subjects are part of their campaigns.

3 Data Gathering

Using Majoritas Social Media platform, we collected all information from Facebook and Twitter accounts regarding a politician of which identity will be kept anonymized.
Both Twitter and Facebook provide APIs for data tracking. If Twitter offers Search API and Streaming API for tweets monitoring, Facebook provide Graph API for posts' tracking.

In addition, the paper's authors considered that the integration of the insights obtained from several social media channels, including micro blogs, generates a consistent image of the political message.
To assess the impact of a message, several data points should be analyzed and correlated.

Below are presented some conclusions obtained for a politician from Europe CEE (presidential elections).

Majoritas concluded that hashtags analysis needs to be performed in order to assess for how many times, politician's hashtags were mentioned on Facebook or Twitter. This indicator provides a strong insight regarding the impact of the message (post) on social media being linked with the meronymy term of Popescu and Etzioni, 2005:

Tag	Created	Times Used Fb	Times Used Tw	Times Used	Used By
[illegible]	2/21/2017 7:51	53442	24431	77873	[illegible]
[illegible]	11/30/2016 15:23	3412	11256	14668	Our pages
[illegible]	11/23/2016 0:51	1245	12441	13686	Our pages
[illegible]	11/22/2016 21:45	25122	23556	48678	Our pages
ChangeIsComing	4/24/2016 16:11	24532	5433	29965	[illegible]
[illegible]	10/1/2015 20:36	5432	45212	50644	Our pages
ChangingLives	10/1/2015 20:36	6453	21233	27686	Our pages

Table 1: Hastags Analysis

Moreover, by monitoring conversations regarding different domains of interests very useful insights were discovered. For our case, the most popular areas were:

Name	Asociated with
Independence Anniversary	Posts, Tweets
State of the Nation Address	Posts, Tweets
Development goals	Posts, Tweets
Global poverty	Posts, Tweets
National security	Posts, Tweets
Democracy	Posts, Tweets
Local development	Posts, Tweets
Bailout	Posts, Tweets
Made In [illegible]	Posts, Tweets
Public holidays	Posts Tweets
NDC	Posts Tweets
Sports	Posts, Tweets
International security	Posts, Tweets
Public Administration	Posts, Tweets
Telecommunication	Posts, Tweets
Natural disasters	Posts, Tweets
Criminal Justice System	Posts, Tweets
Foreign affairs	Posts 2 Tweets
National Development	Posts Tweets
Public events	Posts Tweets
Freedom of speech	Posts, Tweets
Tourism	Posts, Tweets
Ethnicity	Posts, Tweets
Religion	Posts, Tweets
Mass media	Posts, Tweets
Income	Posts, Tweets
Electricity	Posts, Tweets

Table 2: Domain of interests (*sample data)

Besides posts' category, we realized that it is also important to understand what reaction generates each type of post: messages (text), videos, live videos, pictures or links:

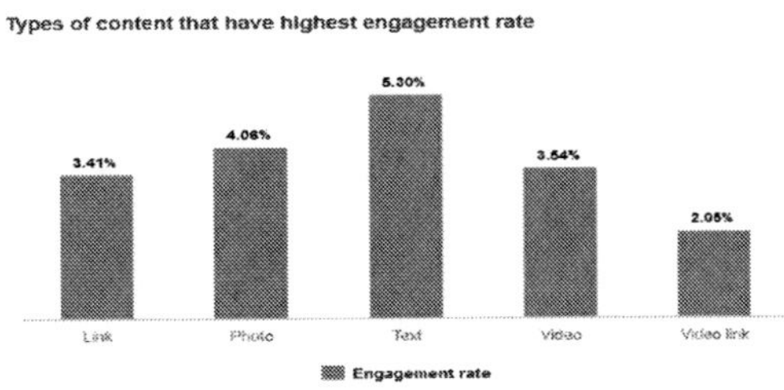

Figure 1: Content Type

Furthermore, subscribers' presence (tweets, likes/reactions, comments or shares) needs to be integrated in the analysis. We need to see how the post reached the subscriber: paid, organic or viral reach.

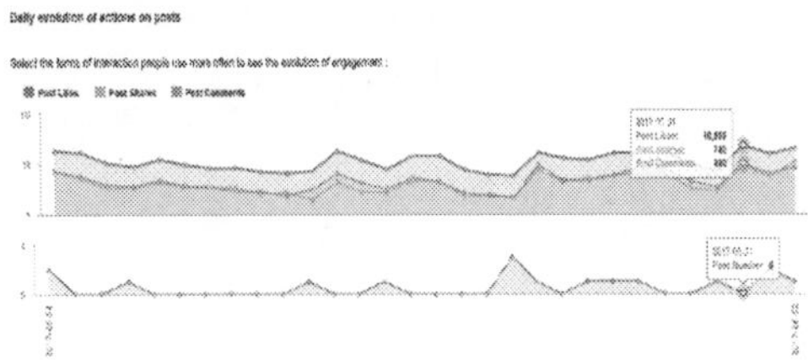

Figure 2: Daily evolution of actions on posts

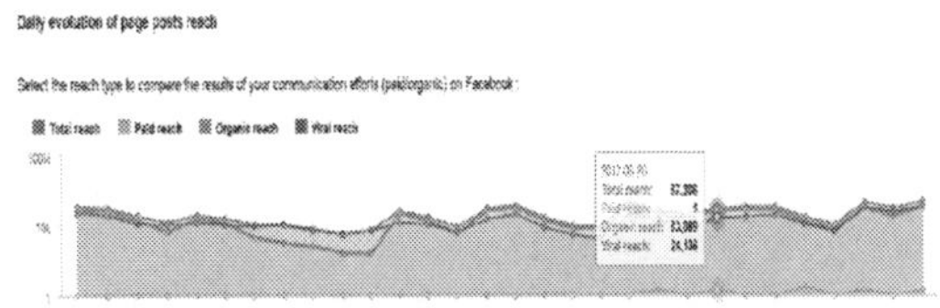

Figure 3: Daily evolution of posts reach

We understood that based on their reaction and presence, subscribers can have various levels of influence [Lazarsfeld and Merton et al 1954]. Therefore, it is important to identify the most 'vocal' followers and understand what are their beliefs. Based on the message that a politician wants to deliver, he can target distinct groups of people and use them to spread his ideas. In order to build a stronger engagement, we defined a gamification process as well.

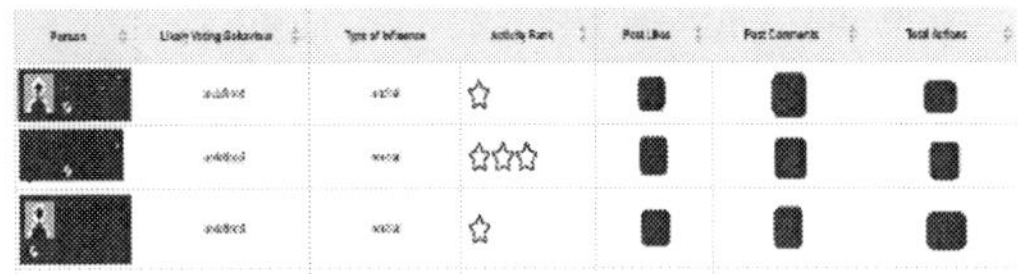

Figure 4: Level of influence

All the above indicators are enriched with statistics regarding the feedback received from subscribers to politician's posts (sentiment analysis):

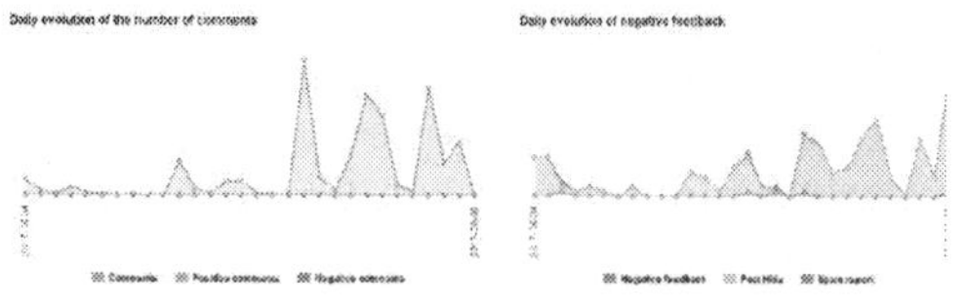

Figure 5: Evolution of positive / negative feedback

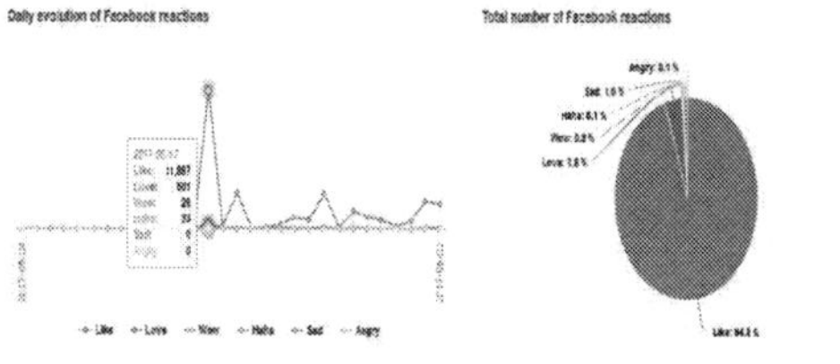

Figure 6: Reactions Evolution

In the end, everything is summarized in a single view:

Figure 7: Summarization

In order to assess a politician communication strategy, it is essential to analyze the competition as well. Therefore, it is important to perform a competitive analysis – a comparison between the impact of a politician message versus his competitors.

Moreover, we analyze what were competitors' reactions to our candidate message (in case they had any reaction), what do we know about their subscribers and what are their evolutions on social media:

Figure 8: Competitive Analysis – Engagement Rate

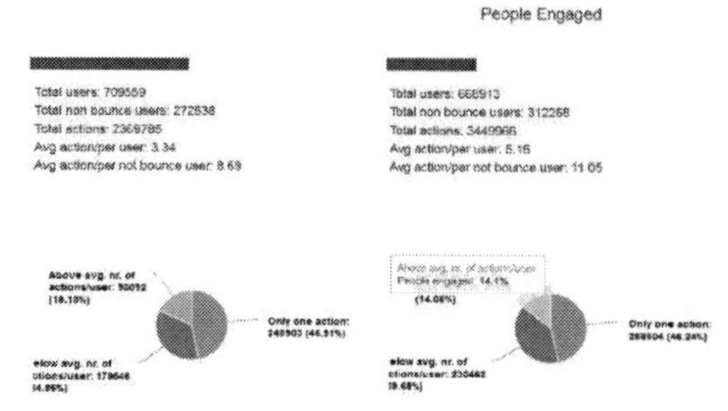

Figure 9: Competitive Analysis Metrics

The application can also perform competitive analysis between any two persons that have accounts on social media:

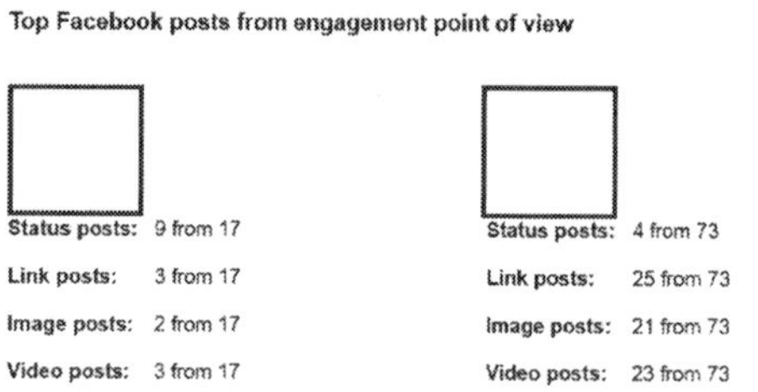

Figure 10: Facebook Competitive Analysis

4 How it works

Firstly, to obtain a proper overview about politician messages delivered on social media, it is essential to perform a strong analysis of the collected data: number of subscribers, number of likes, the reactions, shares, comments, etc.

The second step is data correlation and discovery. In this stage, we identify the main domain of interests by performing automatic classifications. We do a trend detection on topics, on message type, on subscribers' reaction. Also, we outline different typologies of subscribers' profiles and what are their level of influence.

The analysis is enriched with sentiment analysis performed using annotators. Majoritas Social Media Room profiles subscribers through the sentiment they associated with candidate's messages.

Moreover, we create multiple rankings calculated

at a user level: activity rank, type of influence, social media influence rank, probable voting behavior.

In the end, we include competition analysis to get a complete overview regarding how our politician is placed in relation with his competitors.

By using all these functionalities, politicians can define their communication strategies. They can predict what type of feedback can be obtained by addressing different messages. Also, they can have a faster reaction and can apply agile methodology in defining communication plans.

5 Conclusion and future work

In this paper, we addressed the issue of getting political insights related to voters' reaction at politicians' message on social channels. We demonstrated that the political topic can influence the engagement rate and, the percentage of voters' favorability to a certain candidate.

Moreover, the authors observed a direct relationship between the number of supporters than a politician has on social media channels and the results of the elections. Also, we observed that the politicians that are active and react to users' comments are perceived as more favorable. This is trend is not applicable for CEE Europe, but for the all Europe and the US as well (Facebook followers: Hilary 10m vs Trump 22m; Macron 1.9m vs Le Pen 1.5m).

Majoritas Social Media Room was designed as end-to-end solution that assist politicians in calibrating their discourse and offer them the chance to customize their campaign based on people reaction.

Fortunately, there are no other similar platforms that perform this type of integrated assessment.

The automation of this creative process might be used not only in politics, but also in journalism or advertising.

As future work, we plan to enrich our platform with two new modules: one area regarding the prediction on the outcome of political events (there is a x% chance that Y event is going to happen). Another area which can be improved is related to the surveys' assessment: the usage of the wisdom of crowds that perform much better than the media savvy pundits.

References

[Chilton and Schäffner et al 2002], Paul Chilton, Christina Schäffner in *Politics as Text and Talk: Analytic approaches to political discourse*, 2002

[Lazarsfeld and Merton et al 1954], Lazarsfeld P.F., Merton R.K. *Friendship as a social process: a substantive and methodological analysis*, 1954

[Liu et al 2012], Liu B. *Sentiment Analysis and Opinion Mining*. San Rafael, CA: Morgan & Claypool; 2012

[Mullen and Malouf et al 2006], Mullen, T. and Malouf, R., *AAAI: A Preliminary Investigation into Sentiment Analysis of Informal Political Discourse*, 2006

[Phililips and Young et al 2009], Phillips D., & Young, P., *Online Public Relations: A Practical Guide to Developing an Online Strategy in the World of Social Media. London*: Kogan Page; 2009

[Popescu and Etzioni et al 2005], Popescu, A.-M. & Etzioni, O., *Extracting Product Features and Opinions from Reviews. Proceedings of Conference on Empirical Methods in Natural Language*; 2005

[Pozzi, Fersini, Mesina and Liu et al 2017], Pozzi F.A., Fersini E., Messina E. and Liu B., *Sentiment Analysis in Social Networks*, Elsevier First Edition, 2017

[Sundar, Kalyanaraman and Brwon et al 2003], Sundar, S. S., Kalyanaraman, S., & Brown, J., *Explicating Web Site interactivity: impression formation effects in Political Campaign Sites. Communication Research*; 2003

[Tenhunen and Karvelyte et al 2015], Susanna Tenhunen and Vilma Karvelyte, *European Parlamentary research Service Blog: The role played by social media in political participation and electoral campaigns*, 2015

[Yu and Hatzivassiloglou et al 2003], Yu, H., and Hatzivassiloglou, V.,*Towards answering opinion questions: Separating facts from opinions and identifying the polarity of opinion sentences*, 2003

Association for Computational Linguistics
209 N. Eighth Street
Stroudsburg, Pennsylvania 18360

ISBN 978-1-5108-5544-1

CURRAN ASSOCIATES INC.
proceedings.com